William Wake, George Hickes

A Defence of the Missionaries Arts

Wherein the charge of disloyalty, rebellions, plots, and treasons, asserted page 76 of that book, are fully proved against the members of the Church of Rome, in a brief account of the several plots contrived

William Wake, George Hickes

A Defence of the Missionaries Arts
Wherein the charge of disloyalty, rebellions, plots, and treasons, asserted page 76 of that book, are fully proved against the members of the Church of Rome, in a brief account of the several plots contrived

ISBN/EAN: 9783337383930

Printed in Europe, USA, Canada, Australia, Japan

Cover: Foto ©Thomas Meinert / pixelio.de

More available books at **www.hansebooks.com**

A DEFENCE OF THE Missionaries Arts:

WHEREIN

The Charge of Disloyalty, Rebellions, Plots, and Treasons, asserted Page 76 of that Book, are fully proved against the Members of the Church of *Rome*, in a brief Account of the several Plots contrived, and Rebellions raised by the Papists against the Lives and Dignities of Sovereign Princes since the Reformation.

By the Authour of the *Missionaries Arts*.

LONDON,
Printed for *Richard Wilde*, at the Map of the World in St. *Paul's* Church-yard. 1689.

READER.

IT is strange, that of all men Papists should calumniate Protestants with Treason and Rebellions; were Modesty an Essential in the Complexion of a Jesuite, surely they would forbear, or Charity they so much talk of, and so little practise, to be found among them. Are horrid Massacres, villanous Assassinations, or Poisonings, the Effect of Charity? Or, Is Malice inveterate, Traducing or Lying the Fruit thereof? Yet nothing is more obvious in the whole course of History than those diabolical Machinations and hellish Conspiracies of Priests and Jesuites, especially within this last hundred and fifty years; and, generally speaking, Princes, and crowned Heads, have been most the objects of their Fury; and lest the palliation of Villany should pass on the weaker sort, and this Objection any way obtain, That forsooth most of these Contrivances were against Heretical Princes, excommunicated by the Pope and Church, and by consequence delivered over to Satan, and that the killing of them really was no Murther, no more than of Wolves or Bears.

To this I answer, That Princes of the same Communion, as *Henry* the Third of *France*, could not escape their fatal Stab, who never made profession of any other; and though *Henry* the Fourth was first a Protestant, and by them constrained to change, nay, and highly indulging them in his latter years, and as *Mathieus* says in his Life, to all appearance was devout, I mean in their way; yet from *Ravilliac*'s Hand all this could not defend him. We need not long here fix, but look on former times, where for five or six hundred years nothing hath been more common, or more lamentable, than the story of several Princes, struck with the Lightening of the Court of *Rome*, and others wholly ruined by the Vatican Thunder, the consequences being either their own Tragical Ends, or, at the most favourable, strong and lasting Rebellions, which all conversant in History may plainly see; and so dextrous were they in translating to the other World,

To the Reader.

World, that in the very Hoft it felf was Poifon given to one of the German Emperours, fo that Silence to none is a more neceffary Virtue, efpecially in this Cafe, than to regular Monks and Friars, who for feveral Ages have been the very Peft and Bane of Secular Princes, acting not only their Villanies in the Time of the Holy War, but in the time of their Antipopes alfo. But to return to our own Nation: What Barbarities have they not committed? What Impieties have they not been guilty of? What Cruelties have they left unattempted? and yet with a brazen Front daily befpatter Proteftants, accufing them of what themfelves were Authours of; imitating herein the very Skum of Mankind; for none fhall fooner call another Rogue than he that really is one; In whofe mouth is Whore and Bitch more frequent, than hers that is a common Proftitute? And to proceed: What Diforder did they not caufe, to plague and pefter *Harry* the Eighth? What Commotions did they not raife all the Reign of Queen *Elizabeth*, befides the Attempts upon her Perfon? What Divifions did they not nourifh all the time of *Edward* the Sixth, and in his death had no fmall fhare? How horridly defperate they were in King *James*'s time, appears by their inhumane Powder-Treafon; how intriguing they were in his Cabinet Councils is but too fad a Truth to relate; fomenting his humour in the Spanifh Match, a blemifh inglorious to his Memory, leaving the *Pallfgrave* (though his Son in Law) a Victim to the Houfe of *Auftria*; and after by the Match with *France*, how did he embroil his Son! they managing underhand the Queen, and fhe by her powerfull Influence did the King; fo that all the mifchievous Evils of *Charles* the Firft they, like a Mole, wrought under ground, fpotting his Life with that bufinefs of *Rochell*, and the Attempt of the Ifle of *Rhee*, from whence the Proteftants generally date the ruine of their Church in *France*, and by the rifing of the French Monarchs fince that time has endangered the ruine of the whole Proteftant Intereft all over *Europe*, as of late years has been manifeftly evident; and laftly they drew a Civil War upon him, though the Effects proved fatal, as well to themfelves as others, (Priefts generally being no reaching Politicians;) the confequence of which all men here do know: But that which moft furprizes is their Villany in conclufion; for when his farther Life could yield them no advantage, they then confpired his Death; and to that end was a Correfpondence kept with *Ireton* and fome others, not doubting, he being gone, to have the bringing up of the Children, the Queen being wholly theirs, and managed to their Devotion; and how fatal this has been I need not farther fpeak; and if any are defirous of farther

To the Reader.

ther satisfaction, let them read Dr. *Moulin*'s Answer to *Philanax Anglicus*, written by an Apostate Protestant, who found not his Account by turning Papist, as indeed few of them have done; a man I must needs say of very good natural parts, though in several things but ill applied them; and his Conversation spoke him a Gentleman, but withall of a violent and impetuous Temper to whatever he took, and unfortunate in most things he projected. I am the longer on this Character, because most of our whiffling Priests and noisie Jesuites have raked for their Clamours against Protestants about the business of Rebellion, for many years last past, out of the Dunghill of that Book, written not long after the King's coming in; so that 'tis plain, that by their legerdemain Tricks in the Parliament Army they made them mutinous against their Lords and Masters; and in the time of the Agitatour's being rampant, meeting, as they say, in *Putney* Church, they were very brisk in Masquerade among them, several Priests, some as Troupers, others private Soldiers then listed, and though these Agitatours were first set up by *Ireton*, yet in process of time they became so unruly, and so beyond measure insolent, that they were by force necessitated to suppress them, and they were the occasion of breaking up that separate Party of *Cromwell* and *Ireton* in the name of the Army which they had entred into with the King, and by reason of them the King was frighted from *Hampton-Court*, making his Escape to the Isle of *Wight*, which did not long precede his death. Now after a lapse of some years his Son *Charles* the Second, with the rest of the Royal Family, were restored, and let us take a short view of their Transactions under him, where no sooner he was settled, but there came in whole Shoals of Priests from several parts beyond Seas, and *Ireland*, who for several years before had scarce any, and those that were skulking and lying close, was in a little time almost overstocked; and Father *Walsh*, who was a kind of a Trimmer among them, and, to speak truth, an honester sort of a man than most of them were, and willing to introduce the King's Authority as well as that of the Popes, to that End went over with the Duke of *Ormond*; and being countenanced by him, summoned an Assembly in *Dublin* to be held, of the most principal of them, where what a stir he had, and how strangely bigotted those Irish Understandings were to the See of *Rome*, is by himself at large set forth in his loyal Formulary: But one thing which himself notes is not unworthy the recital; The General among them were so strongly possest with some strange Catastrophe that was to arrive (eminently no doubt) to their Advantage, in the year approaching of Sixty six, that they generally expressed them-

themselves so averse from complying with the King in those matters; a violent presumption that the firing of *London* had been for some years in contriving; and the mention that is made of a Plot in the *April* Gazette,--65. was put into the Heads (by some Rascally Priests) of those poor little Rogues that were hangued, one of the main things charged upon them being the Firing of the City of *London*, and what influence their Councils had in that Prince's Reign, is obnoxious to all considering Men, by the breaking the triple League by that close Alliance between *France* and *England* for the Extirpation of Protestancy out of Heretical *Holland*, and no doubt, had it succeeded, out of *England* also, and the reason why it was not effected, was the Parliament's and People's Aukwardness to the War; but notwithstanding they were so not discouraged, but they resolved to go on with their Designs still in *England*, keeping, by the means of *Coleman* and Father *le Chaise*, a constant Correspondence with the Court of *France*, and so strong was their Ascendent with *Charles* the Second, that he publishes a Declaration for Liberty of Conscience, by which, as *Coleman* in his Letters says, he doubted not the bringing in of their Religion; but this so allarmed the Parliament, that they were strangely uneasie and restless with him, resolving to give him no more Money untill he had recalled it, which at last with regret he did. This strangely nettled our Roguish Catholicks, who by this thought their Game cock sure; but being frustrated, used him in their Discourses as if he had been a Cobler, as pitifull, irresolute, nothing of Honour, his Word no ways to be relied on, and not worthy of a Crown; and from that day forward plotted his removal, to make way, as they supposed, for a Man of Honour and Resolution, and who would not be balked with any thing of a Parliament; which at the last, as a great many suppose, they effectually did. And now *James* the Second ascended the Throne, and how the Sceptre by him was swayed, needs no long characterising, for Father *Petre*, with his Ghostly Associates, managed most things under him, who with that Priestly Violence so hurried on things, that on him at last the Tower of *Siloam* fell, and so weak and ridiculous were their Politicks, that they are not worth blurring Paper. Now to sum up all, it is plain by what precedes, That the several Popes and Court of *Rome*, in places where they power had, have been most Imperious and domineering, and nothing so bloudy, base, or cruel, but by their Priests has acted been, not in other Countries only, but in this our Nation too, for since the twelfth year, or thereabouts, Queen *Elizabeth*'s Reign, Popery we may compare to an Imposthume breeding

To the Reader.

ding in the very Trunk of this Political Body, and broke in the year forty two into a Civil War, difcharging only part, not all the corrupt matter; and fince regathering head, and filling up, about four years ago broke the fecond time, cafting forth Filth and Corruption in quantity abounding, the Stench thereof offending almoft all Men in the Nation, but I do not doubt but our State Phyficians will ufe fuch deterfive or cleanfing Medicines, as well as fanative, as fhall not effect a Palliative but a real and thorough Cure, and that the Countrey may be reftored to its found habit of Body. Now therefore as to the enfuing Treatife, it was occafioned by that Hero of Englifh Jefuitifm, Mr. *Pulton*, who being ftrangely nettled at thofe ftinging Truths contained in the Miffionaries Arts, challenges the Authour to make good his Affertion in page 76. *viz.* That the Romanifts Treafons owned by their Popes, and by their great Men approved of fince the Reformation, do far outnumber all the Plots and Infurrections that the Papifts, or Malice itfelf can lay to the charge of Proteftants; all which notwithftanding have been wholly condemned by the Body of our famous Divines: To fatisfie therefore this *Savoy* Champion, and vindicate the Affertion aforefaid, the Authour of this Account with no little pains has endeavoured to give entire fatisfaction: But fuch has the Misfortune been of Writers Proteftant, that in dealing in Controverfies they have to doe with a fort of Men, that when they have, yet will feemingly take no Anfwer; and their laft refuge is generally Banter and Whiffle, if downright Railing will not doe the feat. The Subject of this Treatife is moft matter of Fact, and the Citations, though from their own felves no way unfairly ufed; for if otherwife they appear, let them openly be expofed, that all that are impartial may fee and judge, whether any thing of Paffion, Envy, or Malice, has Prepoffed the Authour, I know 'tis natural for Men, when they have a bad Caufe to manage, to be froward and tefty, and where they are galled to kick and wince, and inftead of arguing clofely to the purpofe, to feek Evafions that may feem plaufible, at leaft to the lefs refined Underftandings, which has been the great Mafterpiece of Romifh Priefts and Jefuites for many years together; for by their little Witticifms and Jokes upon Names, they keep up among their Party a kind of Reputation, not unlike *Jack Pudding's* on a Stage, they pleafe (though at the fame time delude) the foolifh and gazing People; and if it happens that one flip falls from a Proteftant Pen, or a Citation careleflly paffed, that has not proved true, what a Clutter have they not made about it, though the main of the

Sub-

To the Reader.

Subject still remains good. This, as a demonstration, plainly proves the Weakness of their Cause; and had Mr. *Pulton* but candidly read the History of the last Hundred Years, he must have acknowledged that this his great Challenge was a vain and frivolous Motion, and never needed to have given the Authour this Trouble; which being done, it's hoped will be to his firm conviction, and not only his, but any other who have been imposed on by false Notions. The truth is, this Treatise has been written above this year, but such was the Iniquity of the Times, that they would not bear, much less permit its then Publication; however its hoped 'tis not too late the World in this point to satisfie, the only Scope, Design, and End of this Discourse.

Advertisement

THE *Child's Monitor* against *Popery*: written to preserve the Child of a *Noble-man* from being seduc'd by his Popish Parents, now made publick to prevent others being drawn aside from the Protestant Religion: By the Author of the *Country Parsons Advice to his Parishioners*. Price. 1.*d*.

The Countrey Parson his Admonition to his Parishioners, in Two Parts; persuading them to continue in the Protestant Religion: with Directions how to behave themselves when any one comes to seduce them from the Protestant Religion: By the Authour of *The plain Man's Reply to Catholick Missionaries*, in Two Parts: Very fit to be given by Ministers and others to such as shall want such helps. Price 2. *d*.

The plain Man's Devotion in Two Parts; being a Method of daily Devotion. 24to.

A Defence of the plain Man's Reply to Catholick Missionaries. 24to.

Mr. *King* Chancellor of St. *Patrick's*, *Dublin*, his full Answer to *Peter Manby*, Dean of *London-Derry*, his pretended Motives to embrace the Romish Religion; clearly proving his Considerations were frivolous and groundless, and that he had no just cause to leave the Communion of the Church of *England*. 1687.

The Missionaries Arts (to gain Proselytes) discovered: worthy the perusal of all Protestants. 4to.

A Defence of the Missionaries Arts, being a brief History of the Romanists Plots, Insurrections, and Treasons, carried on to extirpate the Protestant Religion, and other evil Designs, for the last 600 years; wherein is fully proved that the Papists have far exceeded any that can be laid to the Protestant's Charge, notwithstanding their false pretences of being free from Disloyalty and Rebellion: By the Authour of *The Missionaries Arts*. 4to. 1689.

A plain Defence of the Protestant Religion, fitted to the meanest Capacity; being an Answer to 125 ensnaring Questions, often put by the Papists to pervert Protestants from their Holy Religion: By the Authour of *The Missionaries Arts*, in 8vo.

Mr. *Shaw's* New *Syncritical Grammar*, teaching English Youth the Latine Tongue, according to the Rules in the *Oxford* Grammar. 1687.

Manuductio in Ædem Palladis: quâ utilissima Methodus Authores bonos legendi indigitatur, sive Tractatus utilissimus de Usu Authoris: By *Thomas Horne*, M. A. formerly chief School master of *Tunbridge*, afterwards of *Æton* School near *Windsor*. This Book is highly approved of and recommended by the learned School-Masters to their Scholars, for their Instructions not only in Reading good and usefull Authours, but also for their Imitation of those excellent Authours, recommended by this ingenious Authour, who may well be esteemed a competent
Judge

Judge of good Latine; having by the consent of all Composed this Book so Elegantly that it's admired by most. Price 1 s. 6d. 1687.

All the Works of that famous Historian *Salust*, containing the History of the Conspiracy and War of *Catiline*, undertaken against the Government of the Senate of *Rome*. 2dly, The War which *Jugurth* many years maintained against that State, with all his Historical Fragments: Two Epistles to *Cæsar*, concerning the Institution of a Common-wealth; and one against *Cicero* with Annotations; with the Life of *Salust*. This excellent Book, written by so faithfull an Historian, will certainly gratifie the Curious, being written with greater fidelity than others; and the Style of it being adapted to the present Idiom of Speech, and the Orations worded in a Style not much inferiour to the sublime Originals. 1687.

The Academy of Sciences; being a short and easie Introduction to the Knowledge of the Liberal Arts and Sciences, with the Names of those famous Authours that have written on every particular Science; a Book highly usefull for the end it proposes: By *D. A.* Doctor of Physick. 1687.

Observations in Chirurgery & Anatomy; with a Refutation of Mistakes and Errours in Anatomy and Chirurgery. Written chiefly for the benefit of Tyroes & Students in Chirurgery. By *James Young*, Chirurgion. 1687.

Plutarch's Morals, 3d. Vol. Translated from the Greek by sev. Hands.

Wit Revived; or, A new way of Divertisement, in Questions and Answers: By *Asdryasdust Tossoffacan*.

The Vanity of the Creature: By an eminent Hand. Octavo.

Guy Miege's English Grammar. 8vo.

Sir *John Thayer*'s Touchstone of Medicines. 8vo. 1687.

The complete Planter and Siderist; or, choice Collections for propagating all manner of Fruit Trees, and making Sider.

The Art of Pruning Fruit Trees. 8vo. 1685.

Guy Miege's present State of *Denmark*. 8vo.

A New Three-fold Grammar, for the English-man to learn French and Italian. For the French-man to learn English and Italian. For the Italian to learn French and English. 8vo. 1688.

Montaign's Essays the third and last Volume. 8vo.

The Gentlewoman's Companion for Cookery and Behaviour.

Ovid's *Epistles*, Englished by the Wits of the Age, with the Additions of three new Epistles, and seven Cuts. 8vo.

Dyer's Works. 12mo.

Dr. *Burnet* against *Varillas*. 12mo.

Cornelius Tacitus in 24to.

Juvenal & *Persius*. 24to.

Mr. *Petit* of the Rights of Parliament. 8vo.

Sir *John Pettus* of the Constitution.

A Brief Account of the several *Plots* Contriv'd, and *Rebellions* Rais'd by the Papists against the Lives and Dignities of Sovereign Princes, since the Reformation.

Anno 1520.	IN the year (*a*) 1520. about three years after *Luther* began to preach, was that almost universal Rebellion in *Spain*, against the Emperour *Charles* the Fifth, which lasted four years. (*a*) *Fowl.* p. 287.
1523.	Three years after, the Earl of *Desmond* entred into a (*b*) Conspiracy against our King *Henry* the Eighth, and had procur'd a promise of assistance from King *Francis* the First of *France*; the Articles of which Agreement are yet extant; whereby it appears that the Design was, to make the Duke of *Suffolk* (then in *France*) King; but King *Francis* being taken Prisoner at the Battel of *Pavia* the year following, (*b*) *Fowl.* p. 301. 302.
1524.	and the Duke of *Suffolk* slain, the Design fell.
1525.	The next year the *Irish* rebell'd, and murther'd many of the *English* Inhabitants.
1535.	But (*c*) Ten years after, the Pope drew up his Bull against K. *Henry*, though he did not publish it till (*c*) *Fowl.* p. 315. See the Bull at the end of *Brutum Fulmen. Lond.* 16. 4to.
1538.	1538. wherein he asserts his Authority over Kings, to plant and destroy as he sees good; and then proceeds with the Advice of his Cardinals to summon the King and all his Adherents, to appear before him at *Rome* on a day appointed; threatening them with the greater Excommunication, in case of Nonappearance; and declaring Him and his Posterity incapable of any Honours, Possessions, or even of

being Witnesses; absolves all his Subjects from their Oaths of Fidelity, and commands them upon pain of Excommunication, not to obey him or his Officers; enjoyning all Christians to have no Commerce with him, all Ecclesiasticks to leave the Land, and all Dukes, Marquesses, &c. under the same penalty, to drive him out of his Kingdom; declares all Leagues made with him by any Princes void, exhorting them to endeavour his Ruine with their whole power; bestowing all the Goods of his Adherents upon such as would seize them; commanding all Bishops to declare the King and his Followers Excommunicate, and denouncing the same Censures against whosoever should hinder the publication of this Bull.

This piece of prodigious Impudence and Vanity would not satisfie the Pope, but he immediately set his Instruments to work to prosecute the design of his thundering Bull; so that the beginning of the next year this Letter was written from *Paris* to one Fryar *Forrest*.

* Brother,

WE behold how the King is changed from a Christian to an Heretick; and how he hath robb'd Christ's Vicar of his Rights and Privileges, by placing himself in his Holiness's Seat there, as Supreme over the Catholick Church within the Realm. It was the late damn'd Assembly of Lords and Commons furthered his Pride, otherwise he could not nor durst not assume it to himself: We have thought of these passages, and do agree, That there is no way to break this Tyrant's Neck but one; Puff him up in his Pride, and let our Friends say unto him, That it is beneath so mighty a Monarch as he, to advise with Parliaments, but to act all in Person; and that it be-

booveth

Anno 1536.

hooveth his Majesty to be chief Actor himself. If he assumes this, it will take off great Blemishes from the Nation, which the Church holds them guilty of, and doe our Business: For then the People (it being contrary to their Laws) will fall from him; also the Catholick Party of his Council will be too strong for the Hereticks, and then the Common sort will be the abler to declare his Tyranny. This is to be contriv'd with the Church's Members, and cautiously, because it is observed that the Parliaments of England have hindred the Church in most of the Kings Reigns, otherwise She had held her Party better than She does now. You have our Convent's hearty Prayers for your Guide.

 From St. Francis *at* Paris
 primo. Id. Jan. 1536.

Thomas Powell.

 This Letter was found two years after among Father *Forrest*'s Papers, together with an account of vast Summes which he had expended for the Church of *Rome* and her Designs.
 * But this Design not being sufficient, the Pope offered *England* to *James* the Fifth, King of *Scots,* and presented him with a Cap and consecrated Sword.
 When that Offer of what was none of his succeeded not according to his Desires, the same Pope *Paul* the 3d. by his Bull of the † year following, absolv'd in general, all Subjects from their Oaths of Allegiance, unto Heretical Kings, Princes and States, as they be Enemies unto the Holy See of St. *Peter*; all Men from the tye of their Heretical Wives; Wives from their Heretical Husbands, *&c.* which was accompanied with a ‖ Rebellion in *Lincolnshire*, under the Conduct of one *Mackarel*, a Monk, to the number of Twenty thousand; against

1537.

* *Fowlis* Hist. of Romish Treas. p. 316.
† *Foxes & Firebrands*, part. 2. p. 34. *Dublin,* 1682. Mr. *Mason* Minister of *Finglas*, in the year 1566. copied the substance of the Bull out of the Records at *Paris.*
‖ *Fowlis*'s Hist. p. 316. *Surii Commentar.* p. 314. *Speed*'s Chron. p. 1033.

gainst whom the King prepar'd to march in Person: but their first Fury being over, they embraced the King's Pardon, and returned home. But this Commotion was succeeded by * another more dangerous, led by the Lord *Lumley*, several Knights and Gentlemen, with most of the Clergy: this Army in the *North* consisted of 40000 Men, well Armed, who call'd themselves the Holy Pilgrimage, and the Pilgrimage of Grace; they had the Five Wounds of our Lord, the Chalice, and the Host, painted in their Standard, and the Name of Jesus upon their Sleeves; their whole pretence was for Religion: in their March they took *Pontefract* Castle, but were at length appeas'd. But † soon after the same Persons raised another Insurrection, in which several Monks came armed into the Field as Souldiers, who were taken, and with the Ring-leaders of the Rebellion Executed.

‖ Two years after (if not the next year to the last Rebellion, for some place it in the year 1538.) the Marquess of *Exceter*, the Lord *Montacute*, and his Brother, Sir *Edward Nevill*, and others, enter'd into a Conspiracy to depose the King, and advance *Reynold Pool*, then Dean of *Exceter*, and afterwards Cardinal to the Throne; for which, the Marquess, Lord *Montacute*, and Sir *Edward Nevill*, were Beheaded upon *Tower-Hill*.

In the year 1546. * Pope *Paul* the Third, not content with his shewing his pretended Authority over Kings in the two Bulls mention'd before, published another in favour of the Jesuits, whereby he exempts them and their Goods from the Power of any but himself; and commands all Princes to swear not to molest the Society, or invade their Privileges; and pronounces an *Anathema* against all who will not obey the Bull.

† Two

Surii Commeent. brevis. p. 14.
Howlis's Hist. p. 316.
Speed's Chron. p. 1034.

† *Speed's* Chr. p. 1041, 1042.

‖ *Speed's* Chr. p. 1044.

* Bulla Quarta Pauli Tertii. Jesuitis concessa apud Hospin. Histor. Jesuit. p. 104, 105, 106. this Bull is called by the Jesuits, *Mare magnum*.

Anno 1537.

1539.

1546.

Anno 1548.	* Two years after this, King *Edward* the Sixth being settled in the Throne, one *Body*, a Commissioner, pulling down Images by the King's Order, was stabbed by a Priest; and a Rebellion was rais'd in *Cornwall*, *Humphrey Arundell*, Governour of the *Mount*, with other Gentlemen, gathering together Ten thousand Men, besieged *Exceter*, and reduc'd it to very great Extremity; declaring they would have Popery and the Six Articles restor'd: They fought four several Battels with the King's Forces, but at last were entirely Routed, and their Leaders	*Speed's Chronicle. p. 1110, to 1114.
1549.	Executed. Yet the next year in † *Norfolk* they Rebell'd again, and when the King sent them his Pardon they refus'd it: after which, they took the City of *Norwich*, and fir'd it, beat the Marquess of *Northampton*, and were very near Defeating the Earl of *Warwick*, whose Cannon they took, and refus'd the King's Pardon a second time, but were at length Defeated; and so were (*a*) another Party, who took Arms upon the same Account, that year in *Yorkshire*. There were other Insurrections in this King's time, which I will not at present mention, only observe what is confess'd by a late noted Authour of the *Romish* Church, ‖ *That these Risings of the Laity in such numbers, for their former way of Religion, would not have been, had not their Clergy justified it unto them.*	† *Speed's* Chronicle. p. 1114, 1115, 1116. (*a*) *Speed's* Chron. p. 1116, 1117. Fifth part of *ChurchGovernment.* p. 139. Oxford. 1647.
1555.	(*b*) After this, we find that Pope *Paul* the Fourth, following the steps of his thundering Name-sake, when the Dyet of the *Germans* at *Ausburgh* made an Edict for full Liberty of Conscience, whereby the Protestants were maintain'd in the Possession of their Church Revenues, fell into a furious rage, publickly threatening the Emperour and King of the *Romans*, That he would make them repent it; protesting, that if he did not recall the Edict, he would proceed	(*b*) *Hist. of the Council of Trent.* p. 262, 263. *London.* 1684. 8vo.

proceed against them with as severe Censures as he intended to use against the Protestants; telling all the Ambassadors in his Court, That he was above all Princes, that he expected not that they should treat with him as with their Equal, that he could alter and take away Kingdoms as he thought good: And one day at Dinner, in the presence of many Persons of the highest Quality, he affirmed, That he would subject all Princes under his Foot. No wonder then that the same Spirit of Opposition to Princes actuate the Members of the Church, which possess'd their Head in such a degree, that upon the Resignation of the Emperour *(c) Charles* the Fifth, *Ferdinand* his Brother was rejected by the Pope; who affirmed, That none had power to Resign but into his hands; and so it belong'd to him to nominate a Successor, not to the Electors: but he kept the Imperial Crown, though the Pope would never acknowledge him for Emperour. With the same Haughtiness did he demean himself towards *(d)* Sir *Edward Karn*, the *English* Agent at *Rome*; who acquainting him, by order from her Majesty, of Queen *Elizabeth*'s Accession to the Crown, the Pope answer'd, *That the Kingdom of* England *was held in Fee of the Apostolick See, that she being Illegitimate could not succeed, and therefore it was great boldness in her to assume the Government without his leave; yet if she would renounce her Title, and refer all to him, he would act as became his Honour.* But the Queen took no care to satisfie this blustering Gentleman, who soon after dyed.

* But the Pope who succeeded him, *Pius* the Fourth, issued out a strict Bull, commanding all the Learned of that Church to find out Arguments to persuade Subjects to break their Oaths of Allegiance, in favour of the Apostolick See; in order to which

Anno 1555.

(c) *Fowl.* Hist. of *Romish* Treasons. p. 287.

1558.

(d) *Idem.* p. 329.

* F xes and Firebrands. part. 2. p. 20.

1560.

Anno 1560. which, he granted several Dispensations to preach among the Protestants of *England*, and to marry, if need were. And the same year his good Sons in *Ireland*, by their example, shewed their Obedience to it; * for *Shan O Neale*, Earl of *Tyrone*, rebelled, but finding himself too weak, submitted and had his Pardon, though not till two years after. In the mean 1561. while, *viz.* † the next year, the Pope's Nuncio in *Ireland* joyn'd himself to the Rebels, publickly assisting them; and by his Authority pronounced the Queen deprived of that Kingdom. But the year 1562. following, though the *Irish* submitted, yet ‖ *Arthur Pool* and others, contriv'd to joyn themselves with the Duke of *Guise*, land an Army in *Wales*, and Proclaim the Queen of *Scots*: to which, the * following Pope afterwards added his endeavours to get our Queen Murthered, as the Writer of his Life informs us.

* *Fowlis*'s Hist. p. 302.

† *Idem.* p. 329.

‖ *Idem.* p. 330.

* Gabut. *Vit. Pii Quinti.* l. 3. c. 9. *apud.* Fowl. *ubi supra* & Thuanus. lib. 44. *ibid.*

1563. But in the mean time, that it might not be said of this, that he neglected any thing for the advantage of his Supreme Power, to keep his hand in ure, † he published a Monitory against the Queen of *Navarre*, declaring, That if she did not turn *Romanist* within six Months, he would deprive her of her Dominions, and give them to any that would conquer them; but the King of *France* promising to stand by her, his terrible Threat serv'd only to shew how ready he was to Depose all Princes that offended him, if his Power had been equal to his Will.

† *Fowl.* Hist. p. 367.

‖ And in this year it was that the Council of *Trent* made that excellent Decree, whereby they confirmed all the Canons of Popes and Councils; which set the Pope above Princes, gave him Power over them, and exempted the Clergy from being subject to them; thereby endeavouring to Depose all

‖ *Concil. Trid. Sess.* 25. c. 20. Decemb. 4. 1553.

all Princes, who knew themselves and their Rights too well to truckle under the usurped Power of their Supreme Head.

Anno 1563.

* *Fowlis's Hist. p. 356.*

* But though the Pope could not send any Sovereign Prince of his Errand to destroy the House of *Navarre*, yet such obedient Sons were the Cardinal of *Lorrain*, and the rest of the House of *Guise*, that they resolv'd its Ruine. To which End they sent Captain *Dimanche* into *Spain*, to get Assistance, there, designing to fall upon *Bearn*, seize the Queen of *Navarre*, the young King, and his Sister, and send them to the Inquisition in *Spain*, to be proceeded against as Hereticks: but this Design was discovered, and so came to nothing. But in the same year we are informed by one of the *English* Spies at *Rome*, That the Pope granted Indulgences and Pardons to any Person that should assault Queen *Elizabeth*, either in private or publick; or to any Cook, Baker, Vintner, Physician, Brewer, Grocer, Chirurgion, or any other Calling, that should make her away; together with an absolute Remission of Sins to such Person's Heirs, and an Annuity for ever, and to be one of the Privy Council, successively, whosoever Reigned.

1564.

Edward Dennum, See his Letter to the Lord *Cecil* of April. 13. 1564. in *Foxes and Firebrands*, p. 51, to 55.--out of the Memorials of the Lord *Cecil.*

† *Speed's* Chr. p. 1162.
Fowlis Hist. p. 302.

† To the Endeavours of the Pope, *O Neale* likewise added his, by rebelling again, and murthering the *English*; committing the most barbarous Cruelties imaginable; but his Power was broken in a pitcht Battel the year following; notwithstanding which, he continued his Rebellion till two years after, when he was Stabb'd by *Alexander Oge*, whose Brother he had slain before.

1565.

1567.

|| *Fowlis's* Hist. p. 130, 131.

But though the Rebels had such ill success, yet the Pope will not be disheartened, but the next year sends one || *Rodolpho*, a rich *Florentine* Gentleman, into *England*, to stir up the People against the Queen:

1568.

To

Anno 1568. To him the King of *Spain* joins the Marquefs of *Cetona*, who, under the pretence of an Embaffy, was sent over to countenance the Rebellion, and command the Forces which the Duke of *Alva* fhould fend from the Low Countries; in order to which *La Motte*, Governour of *Dunkirk*, had come privately, in the Habit of a Sailer, to found the Ports. *Rodolpho* was furnifhed with plenty of Money from the Pope, which he diftributed to make a Party; into which they drew the Earls of *Northumberland* and *Weftmorland*, with others, who, perceiving their Plot difcovered, fubmitted, and begged Pardon. This Defign the Pope was fo zealous for, that he affured the Spaniards he would go along with them himfelf, if need were, and engage all his Goods and Treafure in the Service. Nor was this the only Defign of the Pope * at this time; for in purfuit of his Predeceffour's Bull againft her, he advifed the Queen-Mother of *France* to feize on the Dominions of the Queen of *Navarre*, becaufe fhe was an Heretick; offering (if fhe approved of it) by his Papal Authority to appoint one of the Houfe of *Valois* to be King of thofe Territories; which if fhe did not like, he was refolved to give them to the King of *Spain*; but that Prince, knowing they muft be won by the Sword, declined accepting the Pope's Bounty.

Import. Confil. p. 57.

* *Id. p. 358.*

1569. † Hitherto the Members of the Church of *Rome* made no fcruple to refort to the Proteftant Churches, both for Prayer and Preaching; but this Year Pope *Pius Quintus* publifhed his Bull againft the Queen, upon which they all withdrew from any fuch Communion with us. ‖ In this Bull the Pope calls the Queen the pretended Queen of *England*, a Servant of Wickednefs; affirms that her Council confifted of obfcure, heretical Fellows, declares her an Heretick

† *Sir Ed. Coke at the Tryall of the Gunp. Trait. Hift. of the Gunp. Tr. p. 109.*

‖ *See the Bull in Fowlis Hift. p. 331. and Speed's Chron. p. 1171.*

tick, and cut off from the Unity of Christ's Body; that she is deprived of her Title to her Kingdoms, and of all Dominion, Dignity, and Privilege whatsoever, and her Subjects absolved from all manner of Duty and Obedience to her; and that by the Authority of this Bull he doth absolve Them, and depose Her; and forbidding all her Subjects, under pain of Anathema, to obey her: With this Bull he sends *Morton, a Priest, into England, to spread this Censure, and persuade the People to back it with an Insurrection; upon which, as ‖ Surius tells us out of Sanders, many Persons of Quality resolved to execute it: Accordingly the * Earls of Northumberland and Westmorland, who were pardoned but the year before, took Arms in the North, trampled under feet the English Bible and Service-Book, bearing in their Standard the Cross and five Wounds of our Saviour, and being betwixt five and six thousand men, they grew so insolent, that they would give the Queen no better Title, than the Pretended Queen; but the Pope being too slow in sending the hundred thousand Crowns he promised them, and they at length finding their numbers too small to cope with the Queens Army, dispersed, and every one shifted for himself. † The Earl of Westmorland escaped into Flanders, where he dyed miserably; but Northumberland being taken, was beheaded at York; who was nevertheless looked upon by the Romanists as a glorious Martyr, and the drops of his bloud kept by them as holy Relicks. That this Rebellion had no better success, Sanders, and from him ‖ Surius, give this Reason, Because the Catholicks had not timely notice of the Pope's Bull: And the same * Person informs us, That those that were executed for this Treason, refused to the very last to acknowledge the Queens Authority. Among which Sanders mentions

Anno 1569.

* Surii Comment. p. 770.

‖ Id.

* Speed's Chr. p. 1169, 1170. Fowl. Hist. p. 335.

† Execut. of Justice for Treason. Pr. Lond. 1583. 4to.
‖ Surii Comment. p. 770. Non illos habuere successus, conatus illorum nobilium, quos peraverant, ferialiis quod Catholicis omnibus ea denuntiatio, necdum innotuisset.
* Idem. p. 771. Noluerunt Elizabetham legitimam Reginam confiteri.

Plum-

Anno 1569. *Plumtree*, and others, as well as the two Earls, who are termed glorious Martyrs of the Catholicks by *Bristow* in his Motives, and several others.

To correspond with the Pope's Intentions in his Bull, † *Ireland* puts in for a share this year, where *Jame Fitz-Morice*, of the House of *Desmond*, and two of the *Botelers*, raised a Rebellion; but the latter being drawn to a submission by the loyal Earl of *Ormond*, *Fitz-Morice*, after many shifts, followed their Example, and was pardoned.

† Fowl. Hist. p. 302, 303.

1570. But though the two Earls and their Accomplices had sped so ill, yet * *Leonard Dacres* renew'd the Rebellion in the North, and fought a bloudy Battel against the Queens Forces with great obstinacy, though in the end he was forced to fly into *Scotland*. And now, that the Catholicks might no longer remain in ignorance of the Queens being deprived of the Kingdoms by the Pope, one *Felton* this year had the hardiness to fix the Bull at the Bishop of *London*'s Gates; for which being apprehended, he confessed the Fact, and gloried in it, at his death affirming the Queen had no right to the Throne, being deposed by the Sentence of the Pope: Yet doth † *Surius* affirm, that he dyed a Martyr for the Catholick Faith, justifying the Action as done out of Zeal for the Church, and in Obedience to the lawfull Commands of the Pope: The same is affirmed by * *Parsons*, † *Spondanus*, and || *Hilarion de Coste*, who styles him the valiant Soldier of Jesus Christ, commends his invincible Courage and Zeal for the Faith; and affirms, that his Martyrdom is one of *England*'s most glorious Trophies; though the same Person can afford the Queen no better a Title than the Impious and wicked Queen, the true *Jezebel* of our days: And that all the World may see what they

* Speed's Chr. p. 1170.

Fowlis's Hist. p. 335.
Speed's Chron. p. 1174.

† Surii Com. p. 786, 787, 788.

* Resp. ad Edict. Regin. Angl.
† Ad An. 1570. Sect. 4.
|| See Fowlis ubi supra.

C 2

they thought of him at *Rome*, no sooner could *Thuanus* affirm that it was a very rash Action, but the *Index Expurgatorius* commands that passage to be blotted out; so jealous are they of the Honour of this grand Traitor.

Anno 1570.

Surii Comment. p. 794, 795, 795.

With as great Encomiums do we find the Memory of Dr. *Story* celebrated by the Writers of that Church: This man was one of the most violent Persecutours in Queen *Mary*'s days, for which cruelties being questioned in Parliament in the beginning of Queen *Elizabeth*'s Reign, he answered, that he knew no Fault he was guilty of, but only that he busied himself in cutting off the Branches, while he neglected to pull up the Root it self; which if he had done, Heresie had not got up again: For this being imprisoned, he found means to escape into *Flanders*; but being apprehended and brought into *England* this year, he rejoiced that he should suffer Martyrdom: Upon his Tryall he declined the Jurisdiction of the Court, affirming that he was a Subject to the King of *Spain*, and acknowledged no lawfull Judge in *England*; for which he gave this Reason, That seeing the Pope had declared the Queen deprived of her Right, he durst not acknowledge her Authority, left he should fall under the Censures of that Bull: And at the moment of his Execution, being asked by an Earl whether the Queen was his Sovereign, he replied, She was not; yet is he reckoned among the Martyrs for the Romish Faith.

1571.

Fowlis's Hist. p. 358.

The next Year was that bloudy Massacre of *Paris*, though contrived two years before, wherein (it being carried over all *France*) above 100000 Protestants were butchered in cold bloud; the Duke of *Guise* and his Party did all they could to have

1572.

Anno 1572. have the King of *Navarre*, and Prince of *Conde*, slaughtered with the rest; but they being preserved by the King, the chief Design of the Papalins in that bloudy Action was prevented.

1576. But four years after was that desperate Confederacy entred into by that Duke and his Adherents in *France*, which they and the Pope afterwards termed the Holy League, which had all the parts of a most desperate Rebellion; and continued for so many years, to the Destruction of one Prince, and infinite vexation of another: It was first begun at * *Peronne*, and afterwards formed into a more † strict Union, by which, under a shew of maintaining the King, they took from him all his Authority, to confer it upon the Head of their Conspiracy: Nay, the zeal for this rebellious Association was so great, that they subscribed it with their Bloud; and in order to the prosecution of what they had there promised, they sent *Nicolas David*, an Advocate of the Parliament of *Paris*, to *Rome*; but he being slain by the way on his return, Cardinal *de Pellive* afterwards managed their business with the Pope.

Fowl. Hist. p. 371.

* See the Instrument of that Confederacy in *Maimbourg*'s Hist. o the League. p. 42. *Lond.* 1684. 8vo.
† See the Instrument in *Fowlis*, p. 372, 373, 374.

But among the Memoirs of that Advocate there was found an Account of the Transaction between the Pope and the Duke of *Guise*, wherein the Design laid down is to pull down the House of *Valois*, then reigning, from the Throne, and set up the Duke of *Guise*: In this Transaction the Liberties of the Gallican Church are called a damnable Errour, nothing else but the shift of the Waldenses, Lutheranes, and Calvinists; and it is affirmed that *France* shall never prosper as long as the Crown continues in that line. The whole Platform of the Design is there laid down, and the Pope is to advance that Duke to the Crown of *France*, as the Successour of *Charlemagne*; in consideration whereof the Duke is bound to cause the

See the Account of this Transaction in the Appendix to the Vindication of the sincerity of the Prot. Relig.

See

(14)

See of *Rome* to be plainly acknowledged by the States of the Kingdom, without Restriction, or Modification, abolishing the Privileges and Liberties of the Gallican Church. Thus do we find the Pope promoting the most rebellious Designs, to advance his own usurped Greatness.

Anno 1576.

And his Missionaries not desiring a better example than that of their holy Father, in prosecution of his Designs *Cuthbert Mayne* came into *England*, dispersing Libells to maintain the Pope's Authority over the Queen; and he confessed under his own Hand, that he brought with him several holy grains to distribute among the Catholicks, which they should keep as so many Preservatives, by the producing of which they should be safe, when the Protestants were to be destroyed. In the same business several * others were employed, and one *Hemford* sent over with a Dispensation of the Pope's Bull, whereby the Romanists had liberty to yield outward Obedience till an opportunity offered itself for the execution of that deposing Sentence. And one *Haydock* was employed to prepare things against such a time, and to note the fittest places for landing an Army, as himself wrote to *Allen* the Jesuite. Besides these one *Paine*, a Priest, and fifty others, were furnished at the Pope's Charge, who undertook to kill the Queen as she went to take the Air. And yet these are the men whom † *Sanders*, in his Letter to the aforenamed Jesuite, terms chosen Vessels.

1577.

...'s Chr. 1175.

Nelson, ance, Lacies, iant, &c.

See his Letter in *Speed, ib.*

But our Countrey was not the onely Nation afflicted with these Plots and traiterous Contrivances; for about the same time was ‖ *Sebastian*, King of *Portugal*, betrayed by the Jesuits to the loss both of his Life and Kingdom, which they had before engaged to transfer to the Spanish King, in which they were as good as their word; (though near fifty years

Hist. Jesuit. 244, 245.

Anno 1577.	years since it is returned to the Obedience of its lawfull Heir;) durnig which War, attempting to deliver one of the Isles of the *Azores* to the Spaniards, they were discoved, and treated as their Wickedness deserved; but of this more hereafter.
1578. 1579.	The Pope's Designs upon the Queen's Life being by the good Providence of God frustrated, the holy Father, *Gregory* the 13th. carried on the projects of his Predecessour, (who had willingly lent an Ear to the advice of *Thomas Stukely*, an English Fugitive,) and in hopes of getting the Kingdom of *Ireland* for his own Son, the Marquess of *Vineola*, (where we find, though Popes do not marry, yet they can get Children,) created *Stukely* Marquess of *Leinster*, adding several other Titles, and assisting him with Forces and a plenary Indulgence, dispatcht him away for *Ireland*; but by the way being persuaded by the King of *Portugal* to join with him against the Moors, he was slain in the Battel together with that King.
	But though *Ireland* was delivered from this Danger, yet soon after † *James Fitz-Morice*, who was pardoned in the Year 1569. went over into *France*, where he desired Assistance to beat the English out of *Ireland*, and reduce that Nation to the French Obedience, but King *Henry* the Third then reigning, having sufficient Employment for his Forces at home; *Fitz-Morice* addressed himself to the Pope and the King of *Spain*; the former embraced this opportunity, and sent *Sanders* with him as his *Nuncio*, with a consecrated Banner; and the latter assisted them with Men and Money; the Pope in the mean while raising Souldiers in his Countrey for their Assistance and Relief.
1580.	*Fitz-Morice* and *Sanders*, with the Spaniards, landed in *Kerry* in *Ireland*, and committed all manner of

Margin notes: Anat of Popish Tyr. in the Ep. Ded Lond.1603 4⁰ · Fowlis's Hist. p. 303, 304. · †Fowlis ubi s. pra. · Fowl. p. 305.

of Outrages, in one of which *Fitz-Morice* was killed by the Sons of *William a Burgh*, soon after made Baron of *Castleconnel*; in his place succeeded his Brother *John* E. of *Desmond*, to whom the Pope sent an Indulgence, dated *May* 13. 1580. wherein he highly magnifies the Piety of *James*, laments his Death, and exhorts all the Nobility, Clergy, and People of the Land, to follow this *John*, in fighting against the Hereticks for the Catholick Cause; and to encourage them in that good work, he grants a ‖ Plenary Indulgence and Remission of all their sins, in the same extent as was granted to those who were engaged in the Holy War. And when the Spaniards were required by the Lord *Gray*, then Deputy of *Ireland*, to express their Intention in thus invading her Majesties Dominions, they returned Answer, That they were sent from the Pope and King of *Spain*, to whom his Holiness had given *Ireland*; for that *Elizabeth* had justly forfeited her Title to the Kingdom by Heresie, that they would keep what they had got, and get more if they could: But in a small time after they were glad to surrender upon Mercy, the Earl of *Desmond* having been routed before, and *Allen*, the Priest, who came with the Legate *Sanders*, slain. This ill success put a stop to the Recruits the Pope was preparing to send after them. *Sanders* dyed of hunger in the Woods, and the Earl of *Desmond* was slain two years after by a common Soldier.

And to encourage these Rebels, and to excite to more such Attempts, this Pope *Gregory* the Thirteenth, the same year, renewed the Bull of *Pius Quintus* against the Queen: There were five hundred Copies of it printed at *Rome*, and the Bull it self dispersed over all *Italy*, *Spain*, and part of *Germany*, as is attested by one who was then in the English

Anno 1580.

English College at *Rome* *; who likewise assures us, that one of their Readers in Divinity, before above two hundred Scholars, affirmed, That it was lawfull for any man of Worship in *England* to give Authority to the vilest wretch that is, to endeavour the Queen's death; but that this Pope did excommunicate the Queen we find in our excellent † Annalist, and is acknowledged by the * Romish Priests in their ‖ *Important Considerations*, printed the last year of that Queen's Reign.

* *John Nichols* in his Declaration of his Recantation, *apud Fowlis*, p. 336. and *Reniger de Pii Quinti*, and *Greg.* 13. *Funeribus*, c. 8. *Lon.* 1582. 8vo. † *Cambd. Eliz. l.* 3. *ad an.* 1589. * Important Considerations, p. 62. ‖ See them reprinted in the Collect. of Trea. concerning the Penal Laws. *Lond.* 1675. this passage is p. 76.

But though he pronounced that terrible Sentence against her, yet (as is observed by * one who had been a great stickler for the Romish Church,) he dealt a great deal more subtilly, and more dangerously than his Predecessour; for finding the danger the Romanists were daily exposed to, by their endeavouring the Destruction of the Queen, whom they durst not obey, or cease to hurt, for fear of the Curses denounced in the Bull; he qualified it in such a manner, that the Jesuite *Hart* (as the Lord *Burleigh* tells us) acknowledg'd, † "The Bull of *Pius* "*Quintus*, for so much as it is against the Queen, is "holden by the English Catholicks for a lawfull Sen- "tence, and a sufficient Discharge of her Subjects Fi- "delity, and so remains in force; but in some points "touching the Subject, it is altered by the present "Pope: For where in that Bull all her Subjects are "commanded not to obey her, and she being excom- "municated and deposed, all that do obey her are "likewise accursed, which point is perilous to the "Catholicks; for if they obey her, they are in the "Pope's Curse, and if they disobey her, they are in "the Queen's Danger: Therefore the present Pope,

* *Anth. Tyrrell* in his Recantation, p. 29.

† They are his own words, see Execution of Justice, &c. p. 16.

"to relieve them, hath altered that part of the Bull, "and difpenfed with them to obey and ferve her, "without peril of Excommunication: which difpen- "fation is to endure but till it pleafe the Pope other- "wife to determine.

Anno 1580.

Here we have a plain Confeffion of that learned Gentleman, (who is by them termed a * *Noble Champion of Chriſt, and Holy Prieſt, one that had taken deep root in the Foundations of the Faith, and of found Learning,*) that the Loyalty of the Romaniſts depends upon the Will of man, (except they will affirm their Pope to be more than man;) which is a point they have been put in mind of from *Rome* itſelf, ſince His Majeſties Reſtauration, as we ſhall obſerve anon.

* See *Reynolds* Confer. with *Hart,* Pref. to the Engl. Seminaries, p. 2. Lond 1609. 4to.

This Qualification of the Bull was granted to *Par-fons* and *Campion,* two Jeſuites, upon their coming into *England*, when among other things they deſired of the Pope, That the Bull ſhould always oblige *Elizabeth*, and the Hereticks, but by no means the Romaniſts, as Affairs now ſtand, but hereafter, when the publick Execution of the Bull may be had or made.

Tetatur à ſummo Domino noſtro, explicatio Bullæ quam Catholici cupiunt intelligi hoc modo, ut obliget ſemper illam & Hereticos, Catholicos verò nullo modo obliget, rebus ſic ſtantibus, ſed tum demum quando publica ejuſdem Bullæ Executio fieri poterit. Execut. for Trea. p. 15, 16.

Furniſhed with this and other Faculties, thoſe two Gentlemen ‖ repaired into *England*, ſetting themſelves to contrive a way how to ſet Her Majeſties Crown upon another head: * at firſt they came in the Habits of Soldiers, afterward they went about in the Garb of Gentlemen, and in the North they altered their Habits into the Veſtments of our Miniſters, preaching there, and being ſecretly entertained by the Popiſh Gentry and Nobility, courageouſly executed their Commiſſion; in diſcharge of

‖ *Important Conſiderations,* p. 62, 63
* *Hunting of the Romiſh Fox,* p. 137, 138. out of Cecil's *Memoirs*.

Anno 1580.

of which *Parsons* exhorted the Roman Catholicks of those parts to deprive Her Majesty of the Crown; and the way being thus broken, many flocked after them for the same purpose.

At this time † Mr. *Sherwin* being apprehended, and asked whether the Queen were his lawfull Sovereign, notwithstanding any Sentence of the Pope's, he desired no such questions might be demanded of him, and would give no other Answer: But the Pope well knowing that this Generation of sturdy blades would in time be all gone, for the breeding up of more to succeed them, assisted *Allen* in setting up the Seminary at *Doway* for English Romanists, allowing an annual Pension for their maintenance, purposely for to plot and contrive ways to expulse the Queen, and demolish the Church of *England*, in obedience to the Pope's Bulls, † for which end every Scholar among them, at his Education, took this Oath:

† Import. Con. p. 66. & Fowl. Hist. p. 54.

† Hunting of the Rom. Fox, p. 129, 130, 131, 132. out of *Cecil*'s Memoirs.

I A.B. *do acknowledg the Ecclesiastical and Political Power of His Holiness, and the Mother Church of* Rome, *as the chief Head and Matron, above all pretended Churches throughout the whole Earth; and that my Zeal shall be for Saint Peter and his Successors, as the Founder of the True and Ancient Catholick Faith, against all Heretical Kings, Princes, States, or Powers, repugnant unto the same. And although I may pretend, in case of Persecution or otherwise, to be Heretically disposed, yet in Soul and Conscience I shall help, aid, and succour the Mother Church of* Rome, *as the True, Ancient, Apostolical Church. I farther do declare not to act or contrive any manner of thing prejudicial unto her or her sacred Orders, Doctrines, Tenents, or Commands, without the leave of her supreme Power, or the Authority under her appointed, or to be appointed; and when so permitted, then to act or further her Interest more than my own earthly Gain and Pleasure, as she and her Head, His Holiness and his Successours, have, or ought to have, the Supremacy over all Kings, Princes, Estates, or Powers whatsoever, either to deprive them of their Crowns, Sceptres, Powers, Privileges, Realms, Countreys or Governments, or to set up others in lieu thereof, they dissenting from the Mother Church, and her Commands, &c.* | Anno 1580.

Thus by all imaginable ways did this Pope provide for the Death or Deposition of that Virgin Queen; in order to which he had so possess'd the Missionaries with his power to dethrone Princes, that it was offer'd to be prov'd to the World, "That "the Priests which were apprehended and executed "for Treason, * always restrained their confession of "Allegiance only to the permissive form of the Pope's "Toleration; as for Example: if they were asked "whether they did acknowledge themselves to be "the Queen's Subjects, and would obey her, they "would say Yes, for so they had leave for a time to "doe; but being asked if they would so acknowledg "and obey her any longer than the Pope would so "permit them, or notwithstanding such Command-"ment as the Pope would or might give to the con-"trary, then they either refused to obey, or denied "to answer, or said they could not answer to those "Questions without danger: And at their very Ar-"raignment, when they laboured to leave in the "minds of the People and standers by, an opinion "that they were to dye, not for Treason, but for "matter of Faith and Doctrine, they cried out that "they were true Subjects, and did and would obey "Her Majesty. Immediately to prove whether that "speech | 1581.

* Declaration of the favourable Dealings of Her Majest. Commissioners, p. 4. 1583. 4to.

Anno 1581.

"speech extended to a perpetuity of their Obedience, "or so long time as the Pope so permitted, they were "openly in the place of Judgment asked by the Q's "learned Counsel, whether they would so obey, "and be true Subjects, if the Pope commanded the "contrary; they plainly disclosed themselves in An- "swer, saying by the mouth of *Campion*, *This place* "(meaning the Court of Her Majesties Bench) *hath* "*no Power to enquire or judge of the Holy Fathers Au-* "*thority* ; and other Answer they would not make.

The very same Account, with some other particulars, is given us by the † Secular Priests themselves, of the Behaviour of Mr. *Campion*, and the rest; some of whom being asked which part they would take, if the Pope, or any other by his appointment, should invade the Realm, or which part ought a good Subject to take, answered, when that case happened, they would then consider what they had best doe; others, that they were not yet resolved what to doe; and others positively, that if such a Deprivation, or Invasion should be made for any Matter of Faith, they were then bound to take part with the Pope.

† Importan Consid. p.

Nay, so zealous was Mr. *Campion* in defence of that rebellious Doctrine, that being visited in Prison by some Gentlemen of * *Oxford*, one of them asked him whether he thought the Queen lawfull Heir or no; to this he made no Answer; but when the question was put, whether if the Pope invaded the Land, he would take part with him or the Queen, he openly replied, he would join with the Pope, and very earnestly demanded Pen, Ink, and Paper, with which he signed his Resolution; which Principle he was so rooted in, that he affirmed in the Tower to several * Persons of Quality, who demanded whether he did acknowledge the Queen to
be

* *Hunting o the Romish Fo* p. 146, 147.

* *Fowlis*, p. 5

be a lawfull Queen, or did believe her deprived of her Right, that this Question depends much on the Fact of Pope *Pius* the Fifth, whereof he is no Judge, and therefore refused to answer farther.

The same loyal Doctrines were vented by several other Priests the ensuing year, who affirmed under their Hands to the Commissioners who examined them, That the Pope had power to depose Princes, and that Her Majesty was not be obeyed against His Holiness's Bull, who hath Authority to discharge Subjects of their Allegiance; which all of them, viz. *Kerby, Cottom, Richardson, Ford, Shert, Johnson, Hart,* and *Filbee*, agreed in, two of them only sheltring themselves with this General Assertion, That they held as the Catholick Church held. *Johnson* particulary affirming, That if the Pope invaded her Majesty upon a civil Account, he would take part with Her, but if upon a Matter of Faith, it was his Duty to assist the Pope.

In which diligence to poison the Members of their Church, these zealous Priests did but follow the Example of their Holy Father, who this very year, (as Mr *Gage*, Agent for the Spanish Match at *Rome*, informs us, out of the Records of the Dominican Convent there,) laid out one hundred fifty two thousand pounds, and some odd money, for maintaining his Designs here; of which Sixty thousand was allotted to foment Disturbances in *Scotland* and *Ireland*; so very desirous was the Pope to regain his usurped Power over these Nations.

And it was not long before the end of all that Labour and Charge was found to be the Murther of that excellent Princess, which one † *Sommerville* of *Elstow* in *Warwickshire* undertook to effect, at the instigation of *Hall*, a Priest, who finding this desperate young man to waver, and that his Resolution

wlis, p. 55, 57, 58.

Hunting of the *omish Fox,* . 184.

Speed's Chr. 1175.

xecut. for rea .p. 27.

Anno 1581.

1582.

Anno 1583.

tion was much shaken with the horridness and danger of the attempt, advised him to proceed, promising his prayers for good success; but the design being discovered, *Sommerville* strangled himself, after condemnation.

Anat. Pop Tyr. p. 84

But this was not the only Plot which the Enemies of *England* had laid for its destruction; for *Throgmorton,* * one of *Sommerville*'s accomplices, was the same year discovered, having been employed to sound the Havens, and procure a list of such Gentlemen in the several Counties as were disposed to joyn the Spanish Forces, who were to land under the conduct of the Duke of *Guise*; all which was confessed by *Throgmorton,* before his death.

*Speed's Chr p 1176. 11 *Fox's & F brands, part p. 59.*

Thus we find how vast summs were expended by the Pope; which had the same influence in *Ireland,* where *Desmond* continued so desperately in rebellion, that he swore he would rather forsake God than forsake his Men; but neither the Pope's blessing nor purse could protect him from that deserved death which after long wandring in a miserable condition he suffered the latter end of this year.

Fowlis's Hi: p. 307.

But though the Pope could not preserve his rebellious instruments from the just punishment of their Treasons, yet he would (for the encouragement of others) doe honour to their memories: thus the Rector of the English College of Jesuits at *Rome,* in presence of all the Students, sung a Collect of Martyrs in honour of *Campion,* of whose Treasons we gave an account before; and his relicks, with *Sherwin*'s and others executed for Treason, were kept and worshipped by our English Papists.

Anat of Po pish Tyranı p. 97.

1584.

And because those positions which were found so usefull for the propagating Sedition, might (if trusted only to the Missionaries to instill them into the People by their Sermons and Discourses) be in time forgotten,

forgotten, and neither believed nor obeyed; the Romish Factors considering that *Litera scripta manet*, to provide against the ill consequences which the fearfulness of the Priests, or diligence of the State might produce, by hindring the preaching of the former, caused *Gregory Martin*'s Treatise of Schism to be reprinted this year, in which he exhorted the Ladies of the Court to deal with the Queen as *Judith* did with *Holofernes*; for the Printing of which, *Carter*, the Romish Printer, was executed, and is reckoned among their Martyrs.

At the same time there was one *Harper* in *Norwich*, (a great Friend of *Throgmorton*'s, who was executed the year before,) who though pretending to be a zealous Puritan, preaching with great diligence and fervour, kept a constant correspondence with that Traitor, among whose Papers was found a Letter, in which he desired *Throgmorton* to let him know how their Friends in *Spain* and *London* did correspond, and whether that King continued in his purpose, that the Engagers might be satisfied, and have notice; upon this Discovery a Pursuvant was sent to apprehend him, but he escaped just as the Officer arrived at *Norwich*.

And now was discovered a Design, in which the Pope was particularly engag'd, if we may believe *Parrie*'s own Confession, who in his Travels falling into acquaintance with *Palmio*, a Jesuite, told him that he had a great desire to doe something for the Romish Cause in *England*, by whom he was encouraged, his Zeal commended, and the Lawfulness of Assassinating Her Majesty was maintained; but being somewhat dissatisfied, the Jesuite recommended him to *Campeggio*, his Holiness's *Nuncio* at *Venice*; by this means he wrote to Pope *Gregory*, informing him of his Design, and desiring a Passport

Anno 1584.

Anno 1584.

port, that he might confer of it with his Holiness at *Rome*; in the mean while he went to *Paris*, where he was animated by *Thomas Morgan*, who sollicited the Queen of *Scots* Affairs, when receiving such a Passport as he desired, he resolved to kill the Queen, if it were warranted by some learned Divines, and he could procure a full Pardon for it from the Pope. *Idem.* p. 339.

That the first might not be wanting, *Cedretto*, a noted Jesuit, and Provincial of *Guyenne*, approv'd his Resolution, and *Ragazzani*, the *Nuncio*, recommended him to the Pope, promising that his Prayers should not be wanting for the success of the Attempt: with which encouragement he came to *London*, where he received a Letter from Cardinal *Como*, wherein the Cardinal informs him, That His Holiness did exhort him to persevere, and bring that to effect which he had promised; and that he might be the better assisted by that good Spirit which moved him thereto, His Holiness granted him his Blessing, a plenary Indulgence and Remission of all his sins, assuring him that he should merit highly by the Action, which he terms holy and honourable; to which the Cardinal added his Prayers and Wishes for its success. See the Letter in *Forolis*, p. 339, and *Speed* 1178, 1179.

This he confessed confirmed his Resolution to kill his Sovereign, and made it clear to his Conscience, that it was lawfull and meritorious; which redounding so highly to the Dishonour of that bloudy Church, the whole Relation is by the *Index Expurgatorius* commanded to be left out of *Thuanus*'s History: And well they might; for as it shewed the Pope's Inclination to Bloud and Treason, so it was one of the greatest instances of Ingratitude imaginable, *Parry* owing his life to the Mercy of this Princess, who had four years before; pardoned him, *Idem.* p. 340.

Idem. p. 338.

when

when he was tried and condemned for Burglary. Anno 1584.
But though the Divine Goodness was so conspicuous in the many wonderfull preservations of that great Queen, yet it pleased the all-wise Providence to permit the devilish Designs of the Jesuites to be attended with success in *Holland*, where the renowned Prince, *William* of *Nassaw*, was this year murthered by * *Balthasar Gerard*, a Burgundian, who confessed that a Jesuite, Regent of the College of *Trers*, told him, that he had conferred with three of his Brethren, who took the Design to be from God, assuring him, that if he dyed in that quarrel, he should be enrolled in the Kalendar of Martyrs.

Histor. Jesuit. p. 346. *Sp ed's Chr.* p. 1193. Jes.Cat. p.134, 135.

This Method of satisfying their Consciences with their Confessour's Authority, was so generally taken by the zealous Assassins of those times, that the Leaguers in *France* kept several Priests in pay, who daily preached and asserted, That Princes ought to be deposed who do not sufficiently perform their Duty; and a Bachelour in Divinity of the *Sorbonne* maintained in a publick Disputation, That it was lawfull for any private man to depose or kill any Prince, who is a wicked man, or an Heretick: which opinion had so entirely possest the * Cardinal of *Bourbon*, that because the King of *Navarre* was an Heretick, he had the Confidence to tell King *Henry* the Third, that if his Majesty should dye, the Crown would belong to him, and he was resolved not to lose his Right: But because these Doctrines without force to practise them would prove but empty speculations, the Duke of *Guise* had the latter end of this year a Conference with the King of *Spain*'s Commissioners, whereby he associated himself with the Spaniards against his Sovereign, obliging his party to maintain War against the King as long as the King of *Spain* pleased.

Fowl. Hist. p. 377.

* *Id.* p. 375.

Id. p. 378.

To

Anno 1585.

To promote which Design Cardinal *Pellevee* sollicited the Pope for his approbation of it; and when the Duke of *Nevers*, declared his Resolutions to have nothing to doe with them, unless he had the Opinion both of Eminent Divines, and the Pope too, in favour of the Undertaking; his Confessour, and Monsieur *Faber*, told him, that he ought to take up Arms with the Leaguers, by which he would be so far from sinning, that he would merit highly, and perform an Action very acceptable to God; and the aforesaid Cardinal, with other Divines, assured him that the Pope approved of it, declaring it lawfull to fight against Hereticks, and such as favour or adhere to them, though it were the King himself; he indeed advised them not to attempt his Life, but to seize his Person, and force him to promote their Ends; In obedience to which the Cardinal of *Bourbon* published a Declaration, dated *March* 31. 1585. justifying his Arms, but professing great Respect to the Royal Person.

Fowl. Hist. p. 379.

Id. p. 330.

Id. p. 381.

This Pope dying, his Successour, *Sixtus* the Fifth, was more open in avowing the Leaguers Cause, and therefore published his Bull against the King of *Navarre*, declaring him an Heretick, depriving him and his Posterity of all their Rights, absolving his Subjects from their Allegiance, and excommunicating all such as should obey him.

Sep. 9. 1585.

While this Pope was making Tryall of his Thunderbolts in *France*, he had his Agents privily endeavouring to execute the Commands of his Predecessour in this Nation, for which *Henry Piercy*, Earl of *Northumberland*, being apprehended, shot himself through the heart during his Imprisonment; he had been pardoned for a former Rebellion, and being found a prosecutour of *Throgmorton*'s Design, became this year his own Executioner.

Speed's Chron. p. 1180.

Anat. of Pop. Tyr. Epist. Dedicat.

D 2 But

But a more formidable, because more threacherous and secret, Design was managed by some English Seminaries at *Rhemes*, who thought it meritorious to destroy the Queen; where one *Savage* was so wrought upon by the Persuasions of Dr. *Gifford*, the Rectour, and two other Priests, that he vowed to murther her; to whom *Ballard*, another Priest, joining, treated with *Mendoza*, the Spanish Embassadour in *France*, about an Invasion; after which he drew in Mr. *Babington*, a rich and well accomplish'd Gentleman, who desired that five more might be joined to *Savage*, to make sure work. * *Babington* affirmed, that several Counties in *England* were ready; and being assured of Assistance from *Spain*, they resolved that the Usurper (so they termed the Queen) should be sent to the other World, assoon as the Invaders landed; *. but *Ballard* being taken, *Babington* resolved to effect her death immediately, though Divine Providence prevented it by his apprehension, who, with the rest of his Companions, freely confessed the Fact, for which ‖ sixteen of them suffered death.

Yet did not this deter Mr. *William Stafford*, at the Sollicitation of the French Ambassadour, from engaging in an Enterprise of the same horrid nature; which though he refused to act himself, yet he directed them to one *Moody*, who willingly embraced the motion upon Promise of Preferment from the Duke of *Guise*; but while he was contriving a way to effect it, *Stafford* discovered all, and justified it, to the Ambassadour's Face, who at first denied any knowledge of it.

With the same diligence were the Romanists in *France* driving on their treasonable Designs; for at a Council, held by the chief Conspiratours at the Jesuites College near St. *Pauls* in *Paris*, they resolved to

Anno 1586. to surprise *Boloign*, there to receive the Spaniards who should land to their Assistance: A Plot was laid to secure the King, as he returned from hunting, and another to seize the *Bastile*, assault the *Louvre*, and put the King into a Convent; during which Action their word was to be, *Let the Mass flourish*; and the King of *Navarre* was to be cut off by the Spaniards; but these Designs being discovered, as also another Plot to seize the King in the Abby of St. *Germains*, their hopes were disappointed; in which Conspiracies Cardinal *Pellevee*, a French man, then at *Rome*, was so deeply concerned, that the King ordered his Revenues to be seized and distributed to the Poor.

1578. But His Majesty going from *Paris*, they proposed the seizing of the City in his absence, the Duke of *Guise* designing to secure the King in the Countrey; and for the exciting those rebellious Spirits to some Action, the Preachers at *Paris* generally vented nothing but Sedition, affirming that the King was a Tyrant, and an enemy to the Church and People; and when the King sent to apprehend one of these furious Leaguers, he retired into the house of one *Hatte*, a Notary, where *Bussy*, and his men, fought in his defence against the King's Officers, headed by the Lieutenant Civil: And the *Sorbonne* Doctours made a Decree, That Princes might be deposed from their Government, if they did not what became them, as the charge taken away from a negligent Guardian. And that there might want no Encouragement, the Pope presented the Duke of *Guise*, the Head of the Rebels, with a rich Sword, thereby declaring his approbation of his Proceedings.

Fowlis, p. 3

Id. p. 387.

The

| Speed's Chr. 1195. at. Popish r. p. 85. | The same year * Sir *William Stanley* being made Governour of *Deventer*, and *Rowland York* of *Zut-phen*, for the Queen, they betrayed both these places to the Spaniard, upon which the former beginning to sink in his Reputation, left the sense of his Treasons should put him upon thoughts of returning | Anno 1587. |

owl. p. 62.

Hist. of Treanc. the Penal Laws, 71, 72. f. of Eng. th. p. 114, 5 cited by owl. p. 62.

to his Loyalty, ‖ Dr. *Allan*, afterwards Cardinal, wrote to him and his traiterous Accomplices, telling them that the Queen being deposed by the Pope, could make no just War, and all her Subjects were bound not to serve or obey her in any thing: And in another of his Books he affirms, That God had not sufficiently provided for our Salvation, or the Preservation of his Church, if there were no way to restrain or deprive Apostate Kings: *Therefore* (saith he) *let no man marvel, that in case of Heresie the Sovereign loseth his Superiority and Right over his People and Kingdom.*

And now we are come to the Year Eighty eight, wherein as the Conspirators acted more publickly, having prepared all things ready for their designed Subversion of the Government, and being aided by that Armado of the Spaniards, which they vainly thought invincible; so the Divine Providence as openly declared against them, notwithstanding their

owl. p. 350.

Navy was blessed by the famous Nun of *Lisbon*, and the Assistance given by the fiery Pope, who publi-

eed's Chr. 1199

shed his *Crusado* as against the Turks, and promised to contribute a Million of Gold; to which he added the Apostolical Benediction, covenanting that the Crown of *England* should be held as feudatary to the See of *Rome*; and for encouragement to

owl. p. 350.

those who should assist his Cause, he ‖ gave plenary Indulgences to them all; neither did he stop here, but having provided for the Invaders, by securing them of Money and Heaven, he thundred out his
* Bull

1588.

* Bull against the Queen, whereby he deprived her again of her Dominions, confirming the Censures of Pope *Pius*, and *Gregory*, his Predecessours; commanding all, under penalty of God's Wrath, to render her no obedience, or assistance, and enjoining them to aid the Spaniards against her; concluding all with declaring it both lawfull and commendable to lay hands on her, and granting a full Pardon to all Undertakers. To second which Bull Cardinal *Allen* (advanced to that Dignity the year before) published a Book at *Antwerp*, wherein he enlarges upon the Bull, and tells the World, that it was at the vehement desire of some English men, that the Pope engaged the Spaniard, and appeared in the Cause himself. This Book is said to be written by one *Parsons*, though it was owned by the Cardinal; and therein it is affirmed, * That the Roman Catholicks in *England* were destitute of Courage, and erroneous in Conscience, or else they had never suffered Her Majesty to reign so long over them.

* *Speed's* C p. 1197.
Fowlis, p. 351.

Id. p. 350.
Speed's Chron p. 1197.

Import. Confid. p. 73.
* *Id.* p. 75.

The way thus prepared, the Spanish Armado put to Sea, while the Prince of *Parma* was preparing a great Army in *Flanders*, where the ‖ Earl of *Westmorland*, and the Lord *Paget*, and Sir *William Stanley*, lay with seven hundred English, ready to be transported; and the hopes of the Romanists came nothing short of what was to be expected in men elevated by such great Preparations; insomuch that the * Jesuites at *Rome* had appropriated several Palaces in *London* to themselves, and were so sure of Success, that they would have had *Te Deum* sung in the College Church for joy, upon the news of the Spaniards being arrived in the narrow Seas; and the secular Priests acknowledge the like Disposition in the Party here † *We had (some of us great-*

‖ *Fowlis*, p. 351.
Speed, p. 1199.

* *Fowlis* Hist. p. 352.

† *Important* Confid. p. 63.

ly approved the said Rebellion, many of our Affections were knit to the Spaniard.---- In all these Plots none were more forward than many of us that were Priests.

Fowl. p. 353. With the same zeal towards the Action were the foreign Clergy actuated, among whom *Johannes Osorius*, the Jesuite, preached two Sermons in Defence of the Attempt, and in Commendation of the Spaniards for thus fighting against Hereticks; in one of which his Confidence of the Success transported him so far as to give Thanks for the Victory; but he and his Party trusted too much in the Arme of Flesh, they thought themselves so powerfull, that they forgot one that was above them, who made that terrible Fleet the scorn of the world, and so protected the just Cause of the Queen, and assisted her Navy, that most of that Armado perished in the Sea, or were taken, or burnt; so vain a thing it is to forget and fight against the Almighty, who blessed where the Pope cursed, and turned the Harangues of the Thanksgiving-Jesuite into three Sermons of Humiliation, for so great a Disappointment of the Papal Designs, and the entire Destruction of its strongest Forces.

Fowlis's Hist. p. 237, 288. In the beginning of the year several Missionaries were sent into *Scotland*, to get the Assistance of the Papists there: The Lord *Maxwell* actually took the Field with a small Party, who were defeated: The Lord *Bothwell* secretly lifted Soldiers; and Collonel *Sempill* arriving at *Leith*, in order to the Design, was seized, but soon rescued by the Earl of *Huntley*.

Yet could not these wonderfull Disappointments work any remorse in the Papists, who still la-
Fowlis's Hist. p. 353. boured, by means of the Jesuite * *Holt*, and others, to persuade the King of *Spain* to another Invasion;
‖ *Id.* p. 288. which ‖ *Parma* comforted the Romanists in *Scotland* with

Anno 1588.

with promises of effecting, and sent them ten thousand Crowns to prepare matters against the next Spring.

As busie were the Leaguers in *France*, prosecuting their intended Rebellion with all diligence, *the Duke of *Guise* and his Council resolved to put the King in a Monastery; in order to which, when he went his usual Processions in the time of Lent, they designed to seize him; but being prevented by a Discovery, another Resolution was agreed on, to secure his Person at his return from *Bois de Vincennes*, slenderly accompanied; but failing in this also, the Duke of *Guise* came to *Paris*, contrary to the King's express Order, where he was received with great joy, and soon after, his Party being numbred, and found considerable, he openly rebelled, barricadoing the Streets, and forcing the King to flie, who made his Escape with very few Attendants: Soon after the King of *Spain* sent six hundred thousand Crowns to the Rebels, and the Pope by solemn Letters applauded the Duke's Zeal, compared him to the Maccabean Heroes, and exhorted him to go on as he had begun; but here the insignificancy of the Pope's Blessing again appeared, the Duke of *Guise* being soon after slain at *Blois*, and so receiving the just Reward of his continued Rebellions.

* *Fowl.* p.389.

Id. p. 391.

Id. p. 392, 393, 394.

Thus were the Designs of wicked men, who prostituted the holy Name of Religion to serve their Lusts, baffled and defeated, both in their Attempts against the incomparable Queen *Elizabeth*, and the French King, as also in * a Plot against the K. of *Navarre*, which by the same Divine Providence, was this year discovered.

* *Id.* p. 390.

1589.

But the Scotch Papists were so possessed with Spanish Promises, and influenced by their Gold, and

F   the

the persuasions of ‖ *Holt*, *Creighton*, and other Jesuites, that several Noblemen conspired to seize the King (afterwards King *James* the First of *England*) at his Palace in *Edinburg*, where *Huntley* coming before the others, was upon Suspicion apprehended, which terrified the rest; but being set at liberty, joined himself to the Earl of *Crawford*, and others, in open Rebellion, entred *Aberdeen*, but were so terrified by the approach of the Royal Army, that they retreated, were taken, and after Tryall imprisoned.

And here I find such an Account of the Conversions made by the Jesuites in *Scotland*, as fully confirms the Observation made before of their Design, in their diligent Endeavours to make Proselytes; For Mr. *Bruce*, the chief Agent for the Spaniards, in his ‖ Letter to the D. of *Parma*, commending the Zeal of the Missionaries in *Scotland*, tells him that they had converted the Earls of *Arroll* and *Crawford* who were very desirous to advance the Catholick Faith, and Spanish Interest in this Island, and resolved to follow entirely the Directions of the Fathers Jesuites; whence it appears their main design is to enlarge their Empire, for as the same Gentleman affirms, † no sooner any person of Quality is converted by them, but they forthwith encline and dispose their affections to the Service of the King of *Spain*, as a thing inseparably conjoined with the advancement of true Religion in this Countrey; so that by the Confession of this great Man, Popery and Treason were inseparable at that time; the Romanists being so in love with it, that they made their Address † to the broken Fleet of the Spaniards the last year, to land what Forces they had, several great Persons being ready to receive them. And the two new Noble Converts wrote to the Duke of *Parma*,

Foulis's Hist. b. 288.

Vide Præf.

‖ *Id. p. 291.*

† *Ibid.*

✠ Mr. *Bruce* in the same Letter, *ibid.*

Anno 1589.

ma, testifying their entire devotedness to the Spanish Interest.　*Fowlis*, p. 294, 295.

Nor was *Scotland* alone thus infected; for in *England* the † Earl of *Arundell* was this year tried, and dyed in the Tower, who rejoiced at the Spaniards coming, prayed for their Success, and exceedingly grieved at their Overthrow: And the Jesuite *Parsons* prevailed to have a Seminary, wherein to instruct Youth in such treasonable Principles as his own, founded at *Valedolyd*.　† *Speed's* Chronicle. p. 1180.　*Fowlis* Hist. p. 351. Import. Consid. p. 76.

But though this Island was sufficiently pestered this year by the Papal Agents and Factours for Rebellion, yet were we favourably dealt with, in comparison of the Treasons and Insurrections in *France* against *Henry* the Third, a Prince of their own Communion, who, after the Death of the Duke of *Guise*, was opposed by an almost universal Rebellion, † the Priests calling on their Auditours to swear to revenge the Duke's Death, and railing with all manner of virulency against the King; insomuch that Father *Lincestre* affirmed, that if he were at the Altar, and the Eucharist in his hand, he would not scruple in that very place to kill him. The Rebels styl'd him Tyrant, & Heretick; *and to have his Picture, or to call him King, was crime enough to deserve death; they threw down his Arms and Statues, and practised all sort of Magick, Incantations, and Charms, to hasten his death. ‖ The Parisians wrote to the Pope, desiring to be absolved from their Allegiance, with several other requests of the same nature; and in their * Letters to the Cardinals styled their Sovereign, *The late King of* France, and sent Agents to *Rome*, giving them, among other Instructions, Orders to desire the Pope not to entertain or hear the King's Ambassadours, and Messages, and to excommunicate all that join with him,　†*Fowlis* Hist. p. 397.　* *Id.* p. 40.　‖ *Id.* p. 399, 400. where see the Letter.　* *Id.* p. 402, 403, 405.

F 2　　　　　and

and having chosen the Duke of *Mayenne* for their General, would have had him take the Title of King, but he refused it; yet they broke the King's great Seal, and made a new one.

<small>Fowlis's Hist. p. 403, 404.</small>

To these the City of *Lyons* joined, affirming that Kings ought to be resisted, and they will resist the King in conjunction with the Holy Union, to whom the Parisians sent a Letter, exhorting them to defend their Religion, *&c.* against that prodigal, perjured, cruel, and murthering Prince; the Duke of *Mayenne* refusing to have any Peace, or admit so much as of a Truce, and prosecuting the War with the utmost vigour.

<small>Anno 1589.</small>

To these Attempts and Perseverance in them they were encouraged by the *Sorbon* Doctours, who in a Decree made *Jan.* 7. 1589. * resolved, *That the People were freed from their Oaths of Allegiance and Fidelity, and that they may legally, and with a safe Conscience, take Arms for the Defence of the Roman Religion, against the wicked Counsels and Practices of the King.* Which Decree they ordered to be sent to the Pope for his Confirmation; and this they affirm was concluded on and resolved by an entire consent of the whole Faculty, not one dissenting. And with the same Zeal, and no more Loyalty, they licensed † a Book, which asserted that the King ought to be assassined; affirming, that there was nothing in it contrary to the Roman Church: To promote which they concluded that the King ought to be no longer prayed for, declaring all such of the Body as should not agree to this, to be guilty of Excommunication, and deprived of the Prayers and Privileges of the Faculty. And

<small>* *Conclusum est, nemine refragante,*
Primùm, Quod Populus hujus Regni solutus est & liberatus à Sacramento Fidelitatis & Obedientiæ, &c.
Deinde, Quod idem Populus licitè, & tutâ Conscientiâ, armari, uniri, & Pecunias colligere & contribuere potest, ad defensionem & conservationem Religionis Apostolicæ, Catholicæ, & Romanæ, adversus nefaria Consilia & Conatus prædicti Regis, &c.
See the whole Decree in Fowlis, p. 398, 399.
† *Id.* p. 403.</small>

Anno 1589.

And that there might remain no badg of Royalty to put them in mind of their Duty, the Cordeliers struck off the Head of the King's Picture which was in their Church, and the Jacobins defaced those in their Cloisters: But this was done after the Pope had once more publickly owned the Rebels and their Cause, who by his Bull asserted his Power of Rule over all Kingdoms and Princes of the Earth, proceeded to admonish the King, to release the Cardinal of *Bourbon*, and Archbishop of *Lyons*, in thirty days, and within sixty days to make his Submission to His Holiness for the death of the Cardinal of *Guise*, or he would proceed to absolve his Subjects from their Allegiance; which so pleased the Leaguers, that they reported Stories of * God's immediate Judgment against the opposers of this Thundering Bull.

Fowlis, p. 410

See the Bull at large in *Fowlis*, p. 408.

* *Ibid.* p. 409.

But the King's Army pressing the Parisians, and having reduced them to the last Extremity, they found an instrument for their purpose; who was so wrought upon by the fiery Preachers, that he resolved to kill the King: He was a Jacobin Friar, and confessing it to Father *Bourgoin*, Prior of the Convent, he encouraged him in it, telling him he should be a Saint in Heaven, and accounted an holy Martyr by the Church; which so emboldened him, that with a Knife, given him by that Father, he stabbed the King into the Belly, and was himself slain upon the place.

Ib. p. 410, 411, 412.

That he was set on by the Jesuites, see *Hospin. Histor. Jesuit.* p. 180, 247.

This *Jaques Clement* was accordingly honoured by the Clergy of the League, as they had promised, his Picture was made, and shewed publickly, and they were about setting up his Statue in the Churches instead of the King's, and pared off the very ground where he was slain to preserve as Relicks; and several Divines preached and wrote in his

Fow. p. 431.

Hist. Jesuit. p. 169, 248. 255.

his Praise, compared him to *Ebud*, and affirmed he had done a greater work than *Judith*. The Cardinal *de Montalto* rejoiced at it, and the Pope made a long Oration in its Praise, and decreed that no Funerals should be celebrated for the King.

<small>See it at large in *Fowlis* Hist. p. 413.</small>

<small>Anno 1589.</small>

Immediately upon this Murther the Leaguers at *Paris* would have made the Duke of *Mayenne* King, but he declining it, they proclaimed the Cardinal of *Bourbon* by the name of *Charles* the Tenth; and the Parliament of *Tholouse* commanded all the Bishops within their Churches to give Thanks to God for this Deliverance; and that the first day of *August* (on which the King was slain) should be kept for ever in remembrance of that Action; and that their Rancour against the King of *Navarre* might the better appear, they forbad any to accept him for their King.

<small>Ib. p. 422 423.</small>

And not the Leaguers only, who had been in open Rebellion against *Henry* the Third, but the Roman Catholicks of his Army, refused to obey him any longer, unless he would become a Romanist; nay, there were many of that Party found, who absolutely renounced him, and joined with the Rebels, some few only remaining loyal; by which defection of the greatest part of his Army, he was forced to raise the Siege for his own Security.

<small>Ib. p. 422.</small>

Things standing in this posture, the Pope, fearfull lest any Rebellion should be prosecuted without his assistance, sent a Legate into *France*, with great Summes of Money for the Leaguers, who was accompanied with *Bellarmine*, afterwards Cardinal, and a famous Defender of the Deposing Power.

<small>Ib. p. 423.</small>

To encourage them farther, the King of *Spain* by his Declaration exhorted all to join with him against the Hereticks of *France*, protesting he designed nothing but the advancement of the Catholick

<small>Ibid.</small>

<small>1590.</small>

lick Religion, and Extirpation of Heresie: And the Parisians were so poisoned in their Principles, that the City being straitened by the King's Forces, and Provisions failing, they threw several into the River, for murmuring at the hardships they endured. *Fowl. p. 427.*

About this time the Cardinal of *Bourbon*, their pretended King, dyed; upon which the States were summoned to meet for the Election of another; and for the encouragement of the People the Legate ordered a Procession of all the Religious Orders, who, to shew their Zeal, marched in order, armed like Soldiers, the Bishop of *Senlis* leading them, and their Relicks carried before them; at which the Cardinal Legate was present in his Coach; and the Parliament forbad any, upon pain of Death, to talk of any agreement with the King; in which madness the Parliament of *Roan* had led the way, who decreed, That whoever joined with the King should be guilty of High Treason, and put several Prisoners to death, only because they were the King's Servants. *Did. Id. p. 424.*

Nor could all the prodigious straits to which *Paris* was reduced, incline that headstrong People to Obedience; the Famine was so great as no Age can shew the like; all eatable things were devoured, and but one little Dog to be found in all the City, which the Dutchess of *Montpensier* kept for her self, and refused two thousand Crowns only for its Brains; yet was the Rebels Obstinacy as great as ever, accounting those who dyed of Famine Martyrs, and continuing as intent upon the War as in their plenty; but finding force not successfull, they again employed Assassins, of whom two Franciscan Friars and a Priest were seized by the King at St. *Denis* in a Secular Habit, who confessed there were three and twenty *Idem. p. 428.*

twenty more, besides themselves, who had sworn the King's Death; at length the City was relieved by the Duke of *Parma*'s Army, and the King raising the Siege retired.

Anno 1590.

But as we have not hitherto found a Plot without a Priest in it, so they contributed all they could to the vigorous resistance which the Leaguers made; ‖ For the Doctours of the *Sorbon* finding some Propositions spread about the City, importing, that *Henry* of *Bourbon* ought to be King, and that the Pope hath no Power of Dominion over Sovereign Princes, presently condemned them; which Decree was confirmed by the Legate, and sworn to by the Bishops and Curates. But not content with this, the same Faculty, on *May* 7. this year, decreed by an unanimous Vote, † *That all Catholicks by divine Law are forbid to admit any Prince that is an Heretick, or a favourer of Hereticks; That if he should procure an Absolution for his Heresie, yet if there be evident danger of his Hypocrisie, he is by divine Law to be rejected: That whosoever endeavours that he should be King ought to be opposed:* And then they apply all to *Henry* of *Bourbon*, affirming, *That there is evident danger of Hypocrisie, and therefore though he should obtain Sentence of Absolution, yet the French are obliged to keep him from the Crown, and abhor the*

‖ *Fowl.* p. 423, 424.

† *Jure divino prohibentur Catholici hæreticum hominem, aut fautorem Hæreseως, ad regnum admittere. Quod si ejusmodi absolutionem à criminibus impetraverit, & tamen subsit manifestum simulationis, is nihilominus eodem jure excludi debet.*

Quicunque autem satagit, ut is ad Regnum perveniat,——est Religioni atque Ecclesiæ perniciosus, contra quem eo nomine agi potest & debet, cujuscunq; gradus & eminentiæ sit.——Cùm igitur Henricus Borbonius Hæreticus sit, & si forte absolutionem in foro exteriore impetraret, manifestum appareat simulationis——eum Christianissimi Regni aditu, etiam absolutione obtentâ,——Franci prohibere, & a Pace cum eo facienda abhorrere tenentur.——Qui dicto Henrico ad Regnum aspiranti favere, suppetiasve, quovis modo ferunt, Religionis desertores sunt, & in continuo Peccato mortali manent;——Qui se illi opponunt quocunq; modo, zelo Religionis, plurimum apud Deum & homines merentur;—— si ad Sanguinem usq; resistant, eos æternum in Præmium, & ut fidei Propugnatores Martyrii Palmam, consecuturos, judicare fas est Conclusum, nemine repugnante, in tertia Congregatione Generali, &c. septimo die Maii, 1590. Fow p. 425, &c.

thoughts

thoughts of making peace with him: *That those who favour him are deserters of Religion, and remain in continual mortal Sin; but such as oppose him every way they can invent, do merit very much both of God and Man; and they who are slain in the Cause, are to be reputed Champions for the Faith, and shall obtain an everlasting Crown of Martyrdom.* And soon after they ‖ renewed this and their former Decrees; and when the City was so very much straitened, they wrote a Letter to the Pope, complaining that his Legate had not proceeded with severity enough against the King, commending *Bourgogn*, and other Rebels, who were executed, calling them Maintainers and Defenders of the Truth; and earnestly supplicating for assistance from his Holiness, who, besides what Power he exerted by his Legate, sent them * fifty thousand Crowns for a Supply.

‖ *Fowl.* p. 427.

Fowl. Hist. p. 429, &c.

* *Id.* p 427.

Thus they went on with an excessive Spleen against the King in *France*, but the Jesuites attempting to doe the same things in † *Transilvania*, were expelled the Countrey; yet in *Scotland* their Designs went on, from whence *William Creighton*, the Jesuite, went into *Spain*, into whose King he so insinuated himself, that he resolved to be guided by his Advice, both for the invading *England*, and the alteration of Religion in *Scotland*; which was the Account himself gave of his Negotiation by a Message to the Earl of *Huntley*, desiring as many blanks and Procurations as could be had of the Scottish Noblemen, for the greater Credit of his Agitations.

† *Ob hanc causam etiam publico ordinam decreto extra Provincia ejecti sunt, an.*1590. *sub mensis Januarii initium. Histor. Jesuit.* p. 332. *Fowlis*, p 295. Jesuites Catec. p. 173.

In the mean time the Duke of *Mayenne* solicited the Pope and Spaniard for aid, and entred into an Obligation with the Duke of *Lorrain*, and others, not to admit any to the Crown except he were of their Family; but if they failed in that, to exclude all,

Fowl. Hist. p. 434, &c.

all, who were not of the Roman Catholick Religion: But the Leaguers drew up a Letter, and sent it to the King of *Spain*, affirming that it was the desire of all the Catholicks to see his Catholick Majesty sway the Sceptre of that Kingdom, and reign over them; or that he would appoint some of his Posterity, offering the Crown to the *Infanta Isabella*, that King's Daughter, in particular: And to make all sure within themselves, they contrived a new Oath, whereby not onely the King, but all the Bloud Royal were excluded from the Crown; and set up a Court of Justice to proceed against the Royalists.

Fox. p. 433.
In which rebellious Actions they were encouraged by the Pope, *Greg.* 14. who sent a *Nuncio* into *France* with two Bulls, one interdicting the Clergy, if within 15 days they forsook not the obedience and Part of the King; and depriving them of all their Benefices, if they left him not within thirty days; the other threatening the Nobility, and all others, with the Papal Curse, if they assisted that Heretick, Persecutour, Excommunicated Person, who was justly deprived of his Dominions; which were the mild Expressions with which this meek Servant of Servants treated that great Prince: And farther, to shew his Fatherly care of the Rebels, he sent an Army to their relief, under the Command of his Nephew, and allowed them fifteen thousand Crowns a month; whose steps were followed by his Successour, *Innocent* the 9th, who remitted them fifteen thousand Ducats every month of his Popedom, which was but short; for he sate not much above eight weeks in that Chair.

Id. p. 438.

Id. p. 433, 438.
Yet were not these Designs of the Leaguers, and *Mayenne*, sufficient to content the Pope, but the young Cardinal of *Bourbon* hoped for the Crown, and

Anno 1591.

Anno 1591. and so formed another Party of seditious Persons, called Thirdlings, among whom was *Perron*, afterwards Cardinal; and this Faction also had the countenance of the last Pope, who, to advance this Cardinal, exhorted the States to chuse a Roman Catholick for their King.

1592. And his Example was so far approved of by *Clement* the Eighth, who was chosen in his room, that he continued the same allowance to the Leaguers, renewed the same Exhortations, and declared any other but a Romanist incapable of the Crown. The Parliament of *Roan* published a severe Edict against all who adhered to the King; and Discourses were spread abroad, maintaining, That it was unlawfull to desire his Conversion, and that such as proposed or endeavoured it were excommunicated, and ought to be driven away, lest they should infect the rest; and the Parliament of *Paris* enjoined Obedience to the Pope, and his Legate, declaring that the Convention of Estates designed to chuse a Popish King: And by this time those few Romanists who had continued with the King, became rebellious too, requiring him to change his Religion within a time which they prescribed, otherwise protesting they would elect another of their own Persuasion.

<small>Fowlis's Hist. p. 438, 439.</small>

Thus Rebellion and the Roman Catholick Cause went on prosperously in *France*; but not having the same strength and opportunities in *England*, the more secret Methods were made use of; ‖ the Spaniard was importuned to make another Invasion, which he prepared for; but the Romanists, unwilling to trust to that alone, took a shorter course, and by * Mr. *Hesket*'s means attempted to persuade the Lord *Strange*, † afterwards Earl of *Derby*, to take upon him the Crown, which they pretended he had a Title to; and soon after Father *Holt*, and others, employed

<small>‖ Important Consid. p. 81.
* Ibid.
Anat. of Popish Tyranny, p. 22.
† Fowlis's Hist. p. 354.</small>

_{Important}
_{Confid. and}
_{Anat. of Pop.}
_{Tyr. p. 22.}
_{Speed's Chron.}
_{p. 1181.}

employed *Patrick Cullen*, an Irish Fencer, to murther the Queen, which he readily undertook, and for a very small reward; but his barbarous Intention was discovered, and he, upon apprehension confessing the Design, and who set him on, was executed.

_{Fowlis's Hist.}
_{p. 296.}

Two years before this the Jesuite *Creighton*, upon his going into *Spain*, had desired blanks, to be filled up with Credentials and Procurations, from the Noblemen of the Popish Party in *Scotland*; and this year he received them; the Persons who sent them farther engaging, that all the Romanists in *Scotland* should assist them, upon the arrival of the Army, which the King of *Spain* promised should be with them by the End of the Spring, to the number of thirty thousand, whereof some were to remain in *Scotland*, and the rest march directly into *England*: These Blanks were sent by a Servant of the King's, with Letters from several Jesuites, but he was apprehended, and some of the Conspiratours

_{|| Fowlis, p. 297,}
_{298.}

imprisoned and executed; || The Jesuites complained in their Letters, that the Spaniards were too slow, and therefore desired the Invasion with great earnestness.

_{Idem. p. 299.}

Upon this Discovery, the Earls of *Angus*, *Huntley*, and *Arrol*, rebell'd, but the King's Army marching against them before they had formed any considerable Body, they fled into the Mountains, submitted, and were imprison'd in Order to a Tryall.

_{Id. m. p. 307.}

At the same time, *Tir Oen* in *Ireland*, after having persuaded, and underhand maintained several Insurrections, openly declar'd himself for the Rebells, taking on him the Title of *O Neal*; which by an Act of Parliament was declared Treason for any to assume.

Anno 1592.

1593.

Nor

Nor was *England* long free from open Rebellion, yet clear'd of a Treasonable Generation, who were daily employ'd in new Conspiracies against the Queens Life; for * *Lopez*, one of the Queens Physicians, undertook to Poison her, for which he was to have Fifty thousand Crowns; but being discovered, confessed all, and with two of his Accomplices was Executed.

* Speed's C p. 1181. Anat. Popi Tyr. p. 22. Fowl. Hist. p. 354, &c. Import. Con p. 81.

But being unwilling to depend wholly on this Doctour, the Jesuite, *Holt*, Dr. *Worthington*, and others, employed *Edmond York*, Nephew to him who six years before had betrayed *Zutphen* to the Spaniards, and *Richard William*, with others, to Kill the Queen; who upon their Apprehension confessed, That after several Consultations among the Priests and Jesuites in *Flanders*, *Holt* threatned, That if this Plot failed, they would take this honourable Work out of the Hands of the English, and employ Strangers for the future; that they had vowed to Murther the Queen; and that one *Young, Tipping, Garret*, with two others, had undertaken the same Design.

Fowlis's Hil p. 356. Speed's Chr p. 1182.

While God was thus confounding the Designs of these bloudy Men in this Nation, the Leaguers in *France* seemed to have forgotten, that an all-seeing Eye beheld their Actions, where the Duke of *Mayenne* put forth a Declaration, affirming, That *Henry* of *Bourbon* could not be lawfull King, because he was an Heretick; and therefore they cannot be blamed for opposing him in obedience to the Pope's Bulls, and Admonitions: to which, his Holiness's Legate added another, assuring the Romanists that the Pope would never consent to the admission of an Heretick, that such who assisted the King were in a desperate Condition, and exhorting all to be obedient to the Pope; and when the Estates were met,

Fowl. p. 43 &c.

met, he proposed that all should take an Oath, never to acknowledge the King, though he should be converted to their Church; nay, so great was his Fury, that when the Romanists with the King sent to the States some Propositions for a Treaty, he declared the very Proposals to be Heretical, and by his influence the Doctours of *Sorbon* asserted the same, as intimating a declared Heretick might be King; but the Proposition was accepted, and a Conference agreed on, but with this Clause in the Answer to the Proposal, That to fight against an Heretical King is not Treason; yet the Legate entred his Protestation against the meeting, and the Parisians attempted to make the young Duke of *Guise* King: Nor were things better in the Royal Army, where the Romanists, whom the King most trusted, were falling from him; upon which resolving to change his Religion, his Intensions were no sooner published, than the Legate forbad all Bishops to absolve him, pronouncing all that should be assisting to his reception into the Roman Church excommunicated, and deprived, and all their Actions in that Affair null and void.

But hower the King was reconciled, and sent his Ambassadours to *Rome*; but the Pope, who had formerly refused to admit any Message from him, prohibited their Entrance, neither would he receive the Prelates that absolved him.

In the mean while the Leaguers stormed at the King's reconciliation, and set themselves to destroy him by private Treason, now Force could doe no good; for which purpose one *Barriere*, or *Le Barr*, was employed, who confessed that the Curate of St. *Andrews* of Arts in *Paris* commended the Design, telling him he would merit Heaven and Glory by the Act, and recommended him to *Varade*, Rectour of

Anno 1593.

vl. p. 441, 2.

P. 443.
cf. Catech.
l. c. 6.

Anno 1593.

of the Jesuites College, who affirmed that the Enterprise was most holy, exhorting him with good constancy and courage to confess himself, and receive the B. Sacrament, and then leading him to his Chamber, gave him his Blessing: He mentioned also another Preacher of *Paris*, who counted it meritorious. Thus encouraged, he bought a knife seven Inches long, and went to St. *Denis* where the King then was, but being discovered was executed, affirming at his death, that there were two black Friars that went from *Lyons* upon the same Account. *Histor. Jesu, p. 251.*

It is probable the Preacher at *Paris*, mentioned in his Confessions, was Father † *Commolet*, the Jesuite, who two days before this *Barriere*'s Execution at St. *Denis*, in a Sermon at *Paris* (which yet continued obstinate against the King) exhorted his Auditours to have Patience, for they should see in a few days a wonderfull Miracle of God. † *Jes. Cat. l. 3. c. 6. Histor. Jesuit, p. 251. Sumptum est. de Barrierio supplicium, 31. Aug. die vero 29. qui erat dominicus, Pater Commoletus, Jesuita Parisiensis, in Epilogo Concionis suæ monuerat & adhortatus fuerat Auditores, ne paululùm adhuc obdurarent, & quietis essent animis, siquidem brevi miraculum à Deo magnum ipsos esse percepturos, atque oculis suis visuros.*

1594.

But the next Year *Paris* was reduced to its obedience, soon after which the University endeavoured the Expulsion of the Jesuites, accusing them of all manner of Injustice, of the ruine of Families, and many other Crimes, but insisting particularly on their Treasons, charging them with being abettors to the Spaniard, Fomenters of Civil Wars, and always ready to assassinate the French King, whom they omitted to pray for, while they extolled the Spaniard; that they taught and asserted the Pope's deposing Power; that they refused to give Absolution to several Persons of Quality, because they would not renounce the King; that they had been *Histor. Jesuit, p. 148, &c.*

the

the cauſe of the Death of Twenty-eight Barons, Fifty Noble-men of *France*, and above Five hundred Monks and Friars in the *Tercera* Iſlands, and had refuſed to renounce the League.

Fowlis Hiſt. 443, &c.

Which Spirit of Rebellion was ſo ſtrong amongſt the Leaguers, that a little before the Seduction of *Paris*, the Pope's Legate publiſhed a Declaration, exhorting all Catholicks to oppoſe the King ; aſſuring them that the Pope would never grant him Abſolution ; and upon the Rendition of *Aix* to his Majeſty, the famous *Genebrard* was ſo vext at the Loyalty of the Place, that he left it, reſolving not to live among the Royaliſts ; nay, when the King entered *Paris* the Cardinal *Pellivee*, lying upon his Death-bed, very angrily told thoſe about him, That he hoped the Arms of the Spaniards, and good Catholicks would yet drive the *Huguonots* out of *Paris* :

Hiſt. Jeſ. p. 258. Jeſ. Cat. l. 3. c. 20. *Fowlis,* p. 447.

And *Hay*, a Scotch Jeſuite, affirmed, That if the King paſſed by their College, he would leap from the top of it upon him, and did not doubt to go directly to Heaven.

But to return to the Jeſuites, who finding their Baniſhment out of the Kingdom thus zealouſly endeavoured, and fearing leſt the King, to whom they had been ſuch bitter Enemies, ſhould conſent

†*Fowlis* Hiſt. p. 445. *Hiſt. Jeſuit.* p. 259. *Fowl.* p. 445. *Jeſu. Cat.* l. 3. c. 18. *Hiſtor. Jeſ.* p. 154, 155, 252. * *Id.* p. 252. *Ratus id Religioni conducere.*

to it, reſolved to diſpatch him ; * *Francis Jacob* one of their Scholars at *Bourges* had boaſted that he would doe it ; but *John Chaſtel* who was bred under them at *Paris*, went farther, and with a knife ſtruck the King in the Mouth, and beat out one of his Teeth, he was immediately apprehended, and on Examination, confeſſed, * That he eſteemed it an Act highly conducing to promote Religion ; and that Father *Gueret*, his Maſter in the Jeſuites School, had taught him thoſe Doctrines ; upon which Sentence of Death was paſs'd upon him, by which alſo

Anno 1594.

so the *_Jesuites were banished as Corrupters of Youth, Disturbers of the publick Peace, Enemies to the King and Kingdom; and enjoined to depart the Realm within fifteen days; and all their Goods confiscated, to be disposed of as the Court should see fit._

* _Constituit in super ut omnes Sacerdotes Collegii Clermontii, & omnes alii prædictæ Societati addicti tanquam Corruptores Juventutis, Perturbatores publicæ Tranquillitatis,——toto Regno excant Illorum autem mobilia & immobilia bona vertentur, &c.—— secundùm arbitrium & decretum Curiæ._ Hist. Jes. p. 253.

This Sentence was published after the search made in the Jesuites College, wherein was found a Book of _T. Guignard_'s, which he confessed to be his own writing, lamenting that the King was spared in the Parisian Massacre, applauding the Murther of King _Henry_ the Third, affirming, that if the King were shut up in a Monastery, he would be treated more gently than he deserved; and concluding, that if he could not be deposed without force of Arms, they ought to be taken up against him; for which, and his other Treasons, he was executed; but † _Gueret_, _Chastell_'s Master, of the same Order, was only banished with the rest; in memory of which Fact, and to the perpetual Ignominy of that Order, _Chastell_'s House was demolished, and a Pillar erected in the place; on one side of which was engraven the Decree of the Court, † on another a Copy of Verses expressing the Crime, and discovering to the World that it was attempted by the Persuasions of the Jesuites; on the third another Inscription to the same purpose; and on the fourth a summary Account of their banishment, and the reasons of it, * wherein the Jesuites are termed, _A mischievous and novell sort of superstitious Men, and Disturbers_

Histor. Jesuit. p. 256, 257. Where you may see the summe of his Book, and the arrest of Parliament against him. See also _Forviis_, p. 446, &c.

† Of him see Hist. Jesuit. ubi supra.

† Speaking of _Chastell_, there are these lines, _Malis magistris usus & schola impia, Sotericum etiam nomen usurpantibus._ Expressing by whose Instigation he undertook the Murther.

* _Pulsa tota Gallia hominum genere novæ & maleficæ superstitionis quæ Rempublicam turbarunt, quorum instinctu particulari adolescens dirum facinus instituerat._ Hist. Jes. p. 156.

H sturbers

sturbers of the Nation, by whom that young man was encouraged and perſuaded to that horrid Fact.

This Pillar, as appears by the date of the Inſcriptions, was not erected till the following year; however, having ſuch a relation to their baniſhment, which was decreed the 29th. of *December*, 1594. I thought it moſt proper to give an account of it in this place.

One would think that if any Fact would render men aſhamed, this murtherous Attempt was ſo horrid as to make thoſe concerned in it bluſh; but ſo far were they from that, that *Francis Veron*, † a Jeſuite, wrote an Apology for the Murtherer, calling the Enterpriſe ‖ *a moſt holy, moſt humane, moſt laudable and worthy Act; that it is acceptable to God, and conformable to all Laws and Decrees of the Church;* and in the ſame Book he extolls *Clement*, that ſtabbed the former King.

† *Sand.* Hiſt. of K. *James*, p. 156.
‖ *C'ſt un acte tres ſainct, tres humaine, tres digne, tres louable, & tres recommendable. — conformement à Dieu, aux Loix, au Decrets, & à l'Egliſe.* Apolog. pour. *J. Chaſtel*, p. 147. 156. See alſo *Hiſt. Jeſ.* p. 255.

Anno 1594.

Thus Fruitfull were the French Romaniſts in their Contrivances of Rebellion and Murther, and as willing were their Brethren in theſe Nations to promote Enterpriſes of the ſame nature; for † *Tir-Oen* in *Ireland*, continued in the Rebellion which he began the year before, but diſtruſting his own power, ſubmitted himſelf to the Lord Deputy; yet the very ſame Month he rebelled again, ſeveral Provinces revolting to him; by which acceſſion of Forces he grew very powerfull: And in *Scotland* the Noblemen who were impriſoned and condemned for their Inſurrection the laſt year, having been pardoned by the King, took Arms again, being aſſiſted with Money from the *Spaniards*, and defeated the King's Forces under the Earl of *Argyle*, though much

‖ *Fowl.* p. 307. *Speed's* Chron. p. 1191.

Fowlis's Hiſt. p. 299, 300.

Anno 1594.

much superiour in number to them, but were at length reduced so low, that they begged leave to depart the Land, which was granted them; so promising to enterprise no more against the King, they left the Kingdom: *Bothwell*, the chief of them went to *Naples*, where he lived miserably; the rest about three years after got their Pardons, and returned home.

Yet were not these all the Popish Enterprises upon the Estates and Persons of Princes which were discovered this year; for I find that about this time they employed *Le Four*, and others, to murther Prince *Maurice* of *Nassaw*, General of the Forces of the United Provinces.

Hist. Jesuit. p. 326.

1595.

But the indefatigable Romanists, though so often disappointed, would once more apply themselves to the Spaniard, to favour their cause in *England*; who to correspond with their Desires and satisfie his own Ambition, sent *Diego Brocher*, upon the English Coast, who with four Gallies put into *Mounts Bay* in *Cornwall*, fired St. *Paul's* Church, and * three small Fish Towns; and this was all the King of *Spain* made of his vast expences and preparations against *England*.

Fowl. p. 358.

* *Moushole, Meulin,* and *Penfans.*

1596.

Tyr-Oen having the two last years strengthned himself, writes this year to the King of *Spain*, desiring him not to give ear to those who affirmed, that he design'd any Accommodation with the English; assuring him, that he was resolved never to submit to, or have any Treaty with them.

Fowl. p. 307.

About the same time the Jesuites at *London* had laid a Plot to seize the Tower, and keep it till the Spaniards arrived to their Assistance; in one of their Letters from their Correspondents in *Spain*, dated *June* the 20th. 1596. they are put in hopes that the Spanish Armada should be with them about the

A. P. Reply to a notorious Libell, p 81 82. cited by Fowl. p. 358.

August following; cautioning them to advise all the Romanists of the Design before-hand, and Proclamations were ready Printed in *Spain*, to be dispersed at their Arrival here; and the better to secure the Spaniards landing in *Scotland*, the Conspiratours fortified the Isle of *Elsay* in the Western Seas, for their Reception; but were surprized before they had proceeded far, so the Enterprize miscarried.

Anno 1596.

owl. p. 300.

And now we are come to the last Conspiracy that hath been discovered against the Life of Queen *Elizabeth*, which was the attempt of *Edward Squire*, a Servant in her Stables, to whom *Walpoole*, the Jesuite, gave a very strong Poison, which *Squire* undertook to press out upon the Pommel of her Saddle; but before he could bring himself to undertake so horrid an Action, he had several conflicts in his own mind; which the Jesuite perceiving, told him, * That the Sin of Backsliding did seldom obtain pardon, and if he did but once doubt of the lawfulness, or merit, of the Act, it was enough to cast him down to Hell; exhorting him to go through with it; † for if he failed, he would commit an unpardonable Sin before God; and at parting, after having bless'd him, he used these words, *My Son, God bless thee, and make thee strong; be of good courage; I pawn my Soul for thine; and being either dead or alive, assure thy self thou shalt have part of my Prayers.*

1597.

pred. p. 1183.
owl. p. 357.
mport. Conj. p. 81.
inat. of Pop.
Tyran. *p.* 26.

Speed, p. 183.

ef. Cat. l 3.
. 4

Thus satisfied with the Jesuites, he, upon the first opportunity, poisoned the Pommel of the Queens Saddle, but it pleased God the Poison had not the expected effect; upon which the Jesuites not hearing of her Death in some time, suspected *Squire* of Unfaithfulness, and got him under-hand accused of some Design against the Queen; upon which being apprehended he confessed all, and was executed.

But

Anno 1597.

But *Tyrone* created more trouble to the Queen in *Speed*, p. 1121, *Ireland*, where daily he encreased his strength, took 1122. fortified Places from the English, and in several Skirmishes got the better of the Queens Forces.

1598.

And continuing his Rebellion, slew Sir *Henry* *Id.* p. 1123. *Bagnall*, and routed the English under his Command, took the Fort of *Black-water*, and in it great store of Ammunition and Arms, and created *James Fitz-Thomas* Earl of *Desmond*, and got several Advantages over the Forces of the Kingdom.

In *England Anthony Rolston* was employed by *Cambd.* Annal. the Jesuite *Creswell* to prepare things for an Invasion, which the Spaniard intended to make very suddenly; in order to which a Fleet was prepared, and a Proclamation drawn up by the Admiral, justifying the Action, and declaring his Intention to be, *to reduce these Kingdoms to the Obedience of the Catholick Roman Church.*

This year also was apprehended in *Holland* one *Peter Pan*, a Cooper of *Ipres*, who confess'd, That his Design was to murther Prince *Maurice* of *Nassaw*, * that the Jesuites of *Doway*, for his encourage- * *Jes. Catec.* ment, promised to make his Son a Prebend, and the l. 3. c 1. Provincial gave him his Blessing in these Words, *Hist. Jes.* p. 336. *Friend, go thy ways in peace, for thou goest as an Angel under God's safeguard and protection.*

But almost innumerable were the Conspiracies against King *Henry* of *France*, against whom (after *Fowl.* p. 449, *Mayenne* and all others had submitted) the Dukes 450. of *Aumale*, and *Mercent* continued obstinate, refusing to acknowledge him; and the Pope's Agent at *Brussels*, first employed *Ridicove*, a Dominican of *Ghent*, to murther the King; assuring him, That the Pope and Cardinals approved of the Action; but he, after two Journeys into *France* about it, was apprehended, and executed; confessing, *That the daily*

daily Sermons he had heard in praise of Clement, *who stabb'd the former King, and was esteemed a Martyr among them, had so enflam'd him, that he resolv'd to follow his steps.* Besides this Man, one *Arger*, of the same Order, undertook the same Exploit; to whom the Pope's Agent added *Clement Odin*, another Son of St. *Dominick*; but God defeated all their Designs, and preserv'd that great King's Life some years longer.

Fow. p. 308.
Speed. p. 1225.

In the mean while *Tir Oen* continued his Rebellion in *Ireland*, having received Assistance from the Spaniard, and a Plume of Phœnix Feathers from the Pope; and the new Earl of *Desmond* wrote two * Letters to the King of *Spain*, begging his Assistance to drive the English out of *Ireland*, and to advance the Catholick Cause, which he was resolved to maintain. What effect these and other Addresses had, we shall see presently.

* See them at large in *Fowlis,* p. 308. 309.

But *Tir Oen* not resting wholly on the Spaniard, wrote a very earnest Letter to the Pope, subscribed by himself, *Desmond*, and others; † *Desiring his Holiness to issue out a Bull against the Queen*, as Pius the Fifth, and Gregory the Thirteenth had done; which they press him to doe, *because the Kingdom belonged to his Holiness, and next under God depended solely on him.*

† *Desideramus ut quemadmodum fælicis recordationis* Pius V. P. M. *contra Reginam Angliæ----Bullam excommunicationis ediderat, necnon* Greg. 13. *eandem continuaverat---- Similem quoque sententiam ad hoc bellum promovendum, & ad fœlicem exitum deducendum sanctitas vestra emittere dignetur.* Fowl. p. 478.

In the mean while, the Rebellion went on, and daily conflicts happen'd; but lest the tediousness, or danger of the War should discourage them, Pope Clement the Eighth sent a Letter, directed to all the Prelates, Noblemen, and People of *Ireland*, wherein ‖ he owns, That they had taken up Arms by his advice, for recovering their Liberty, and opposing

‖ *Cùm vos Rom. Pontificum prædecessorum nostrorum, & no-*

Anno 1598.

1599.

1600.

Anno 1600.

posing the Hereticks, commends the *Fitz-Geralds* who headed former Insurrections, highly extolls *Tyrone*, and grants a full remission of all Sins to him and his Assistants.

ſtris & Apoſto-licæ ſedis co-hortationibus adductis
——Hugoni O Neale——
conjunctis animis & viribus præſto fueritis. See the Letter at large in *Fowlis*, p. 479, 480.

Yet could not this Concurrence, and Benediction of the Pope preserve their strength from being broken by the Lord *Mountjoy*, who this year arrived Lord Deputy in *Ireland*; insomuch that several of the chief Rebels submitted, * but at the same time sent to *Rome* to crave Pardon for their outward compliance: but *Tyrone* continued obstinate, which forced the Lord-Deputy to proclaim him Traitor, setting a Reward of Two thousand Marks upon his Head; however the Spaniard sent a Ship to his Relief, laden with Arms and Monies, as an earnest of more Supplies.

Speed, p. 1125, 1126.

* *Fowlis* p. 480.

This year Col. *Sempill* betrayed *Lyer* in *Flanders* to the Spaniards. *Wadſw. Engl. Span. Pilgr.* p 61. *Lond.* 1630. ---4to.

It is certain from the Confession of the Traitors themselves, that the foundation of the Gun-powder Treason was laid the following year; but it is very probable that there was a rough draught of it made in this, as appears by the Case resolv'd by *Delrio* the Jesuite; whether if one discover in Confession, that he hath laid Gun-powder under an House, by which the House is to be blown up, and the Prince destroyed, the Priest ought to reveal it? upon which he concludes, that he ought not; it was a Case that had never happened before and so not likely to have been thought of by a Person not cautious of such a Design; and this Resolution *Garnet* after served himself of, alledging, That all the Knowledge he had of the Treason was communicated to him in Confession, which he was bound not to disclose, upon any Account whatsoever.

Delr. Diſquis. Magi. l. 6. c. 1. *Lov.* 1600. 4to.

Account of the Proceedings against the Gunp. Trait. p. 215. *Lond.* 1679. 8to.

Soon.

Soon after his last Letter in *Tyrone*'s behalf, the same Pope sent his *Breves* into *England*, commanding all the Roman Catholicks not to admit, after the Queen's death, any Prince whatsoever, unless he would bind himself by Oath to promote the Roman Catholick Religion to his utmost Power: In prosecution of which, knowing that King *James*, the next Successour, was a firm Protestant, several Designs were formed against his Life; *Hay* and *Hamilton*, two Papists, were sent into *Scotland*, to stir up the Jesuites there, who were received and cherished, notwithstanding the King had by his Proclamation forbidden any to harbour them, affirming that if any did, he would look upon them as Designers against his Life.

Foxes & Firebrands, pt. 2, p. 52. Fowl. p. 499. Acct. of the Proceedings against the Gunpowder Trait. p. 159.

Foxes & Firebrands, ubi supra.

But while these Jesuites, and others of the same stamp, were endeavouring to prepare matters for a Rebellion, one ‖ *Mowbray*, Son to a Scotch Nobleman, undertook to destroy the King, but was apprehended at *London*, and sent Prisoner into *Scotland* by the Queen; and about the same time the * Duke of *Tuscany*, by some Letters he had intercepted, discovered another Design against his Life, which was to be effected by Poison, an Account of which he sent immediately to the King by Sir *Henry Wotton*, then in his Court, with several Antidotes against the Poison, if it should be given him, notwithstanding all his diligence to prevent it.

‖ *Fowlis's Hist. p. 498.*

* *Walton's Life of Sir Henry Wotton, p. 104, &c.*

During these Designs in *Scotland* the Pope sent a Letter to *Tyrone*, calling his Rebellion an † *Holy League*, ‖ assuring him that he was *exceedingly pleased at their Courage and Zeal*, extolling his *Piety, in Domino cepimus.*——*Laudamus egregiam pietatem & fortitudinem tuam.*——*Conservate filii hanc Mentem, conservate Unionem,*——*& Deus erit vobiscum, & pugnabit pro vobis. Ubi opus erit, scribemus efficaciter ad Reges & Principes Catholicos,*—— *ut vobis & Confoederatis omni ope suffragentur. Cogitamus etiam propediem mittere ad vos peculiarem nuncium nostrum. Tibi & cæteris qui tibi unanimes pro fidei Catholicæ Propugnatione adhæreunt, ut Illam & Apostolicam benedictionem benigne impertimur.* Fowl. p. 482.

† *Sacrum fœdus quod tu & Principes, &c.*

‖ *Magnam ex his voluptatem*

Anno 1601.

ety, *exhorting him to go on as he had begun, and praying that God would fight for him; promising to write to all Catholick Princes to assist him, and to send a Nuncio to reside with him; and giving his Blessing to him and all his Followers, who should hazard themselves for the Catholick Cause.*

Besides which he sent a † *Breve* to the whole Body of the Irish Nation, requiring them to join with *Tyr-Oen* against the Queen; and if we may believe * *Don Juan de Aquila*, General of the War in *Ireland* for defence of the Faith, he went farther than this, and excommunicated, and (as far as in him lay) deposed Her Majesty.

† *Walsh*'s Hist of the Irish Rem. Pref. p. 11.
* See his Declaration in *Fowlis* Hist. p 484, &c.

This Spanish Commander arrived at *Kingsall* with a great Fleet, and began to fortifie the Town; and published a Declaration, affirming, That the War made against Queen *Elizabeth* by his Master, in Conjunction with *Tyr-Oen*, was just, She having been excommunicated, and her Subjects absolved from their Fidelity by several Popes; exhorting them, that now Christ's Vicar commanded them, they would in obedience to him take Arms; protesting, that if any continued in obedience to the English, they should be prosecuted as Hereticks, and hatefull Enemies of the Church.

Speed's Chr. p. 1226.

Soon after *Don Alonso del Campo* landed with a Supply of Soldiers, but suddenly after his arrival was taken Prisoner, the Army of the Spaniards and Rebells in conjunction routed, and the former glad to be permitted to return home.

Fowlis's Hist. p. 486.
Speed's Chr. p. 1226.

Yet were the English Papists as diligent as ever to introduce the Spaniards, and therefore dispatched away ‖ *Thomas Winter*, to trie what could be done for their assistance, who were ready to sacrifice their Lives for the Catholick Cause; and to assure the King of *Spain*, that if he would send over an Army,

‖ Hist of the Gunpow. Tr. p. 2, 3.

I   they

they would have in a readineſs Fifteen hundred or two thouſand Horſes for the Service; being introduced by the means of the Jeſuite *Creſwell,* the Duke of *Lerma* aſſured him of Aſſiſtance, and the Count *de Miranda* told him, that his Maſter would beſtow two hundred thouſand Crowns for that uſe, and would have an Army in *England* by the next Spring.

Anno 1601.

With this gratefull Account of the poſture of Affairs he returned, and great preparations were made, that they might be ready againſt the arrival of the Forces; but all their meaſures were broken by the Queen's death, yet was Mr. *Wright* ſent into *Spain,* and *Guy Faux* after him; but the King refuſed to meddle, having ſent his Ambaſſadour to conclude a Peace with King *James*; upon which diſappointment they entertained new Deſigns, which we ſhall have account of in a little time.

1602.

Hiſt. Gunp. Tr. p. 3.

While theſe Matters were tranſacting in *Spain* and *England, Tyr-Oen* and *Oſulevan* continued their Inſurrection in *Ireland,* the latter keeping the Caſtle of *Dunboy* for the King of *Spain,* to whom he ſent to deſire him to accept it, which he did, and ſent *Oſulevan* twelve thouſand pounds, with a ſupply of Arms and Ammunition; and the reſt of the Rebells received Encouragement from their Correſpondents in *Spain,* who aſſured them, his Catholick Majeſty would not omit the winning of *Ireland,* if it coſt him the moſt part of *Spain*; and that an Army of fourteen thouſand men, with a Nuncio from the Pope, were ſet Sail for their Relief, which News rendered them ſo obſtinate, that they endured all Extremities; but the taking of *Dunboy* by the Lord Deputy put a ſtop to thoſe ſuccours, there being no place for to receive them at their landing; yet did *Mac Eggan,* the Apoſtolical Vicar, revive the fury of the Rebells, but he was ſlain the latter end

Fowl. Hiſt. p. 486, &c.

Anno 1602. of this year, fighting at the head of his Men, with a Sword drawn in one hand, and his Breviary and Beads in the other.

We have seen the Pope approving this Rebellion, so that the Divines of his Church could doe no less than follow the Dictates of their Supreme Head, which the Jesuites of *Salamanca* did this year by a Declaration of theirs; in which they resolve, * *That we must hold for certain that the Pope hath power to bridle and suppress those who forsake the Faith:* And having farther stated the Question, they proceed to affirm, *That it is lawfull for any Catholick to assist* Tyr-Oen, *and that with great Merit, and good Hope of eternal Reward, because it is by the Pope's Authority, that all such Romanists as take part with the English sin mortally, and cannot be saved, or receive Absolution, till they forsake the English Army; and those are in the same condition who give the English any Tribute, except such as the Pope hath given them leave to pay,* (so that they are to be Subjects no longer than the Pope pleases.) And then they proceed to shew, *That the Bull in favour of the Rebells was not procured by surreption, but proceeded from the Pope's own Inclination to them, and that the permission given to the Roman Catholicks to obey her, extended only to such Obedience as doth not oppugn the Catholick Religion, which the assisting Her against* Tyrone *doth.* And this Declaration is dated the seventh of *March.* 1602.

* *Tanquam certum est accipiendum, posse Rom. Pontif. fidei desertores, armis compellere ac coercere;-- posse quoscunque Catholicos Hugoni O Neal in præd. bello favere, idque magno cum merito, & spe maxima retributionis æternæ; cùm enim bellum gerit authoritate summi Pontificis.--- Eos omnes Catholicos peccare mortaliter, qui Anglorum castra — sequuntur; nec posse illos æternam salutem consequi, nec ullo Sacerdote à suis peccatis absolvi, nisi priùs respiscant, ac Castra Anglorum deserant. Idémque de illis censendum est qui illis tribuunt, præterea Tributa consueta quæ ex Summi Pont. Indulgentia & Permissione eis licet Anglis Regibus — solvere — Surreptio intervenire non potest, nulla narratur Petitio eorum in quorum favorem expeditur; at Summus Pont. apertè in illis literis docet se & Antecessores suos sponte exhortatos fuisse ad illud bellum gerendum Hibernos.---Permissum est etiam Catholicis Hæreticæ Reginæ id genus obsequii præstare quod Catholicam Religionem non oppugnet.— Datum Salamanticæ, 7. Martii. 1602.*

And it could be nothing less than such an extraordinary encouragement, that could render the Irish so audacious as they were upon the Queen's Death; in *Limrick* they seized the Churches, and set up Mass in them; the same they did at *Waterford*, in the Cathedral, and at the Sessions House they pulled down the Seats of Justice; in *Cork* they refused to proclaim the King, and by Force opposed the Commissioners; they went in a solemn Procession, took the Sacrament to spend their Lives in defence of the Roman Catholick Religion; wrote to several Cities to assist them, seized upon the King's stores, and assaulted his Forces, alledging that he could not be lawfull King, because he was not appointed by the Pope.

Fowl. p. 435.

Anno 1602.

And for their farther satisfaction the University of *Salamanca*, subscribed the Declaration which the Jesuites made the year before; and the Divines of *Valedolid* did the same.

Fowl. p. 494.
Hist. of the Irish Remon.
Pref. p. 11.

1603.

About this time the Jesuites laboured to get the Sentence of their Banishment out of *France* reversed, the Pope interposing his Mediation in their Favours, upon which the Parliament of *Paris* attempted to disswade the King from consenting to it by a long * Oration; alledging, *That it was their avowed Doctrine, That the Pope hath a Power of Excommunicating Kings; that a King so Excommunicated by his Holiness, is no other than a Tyrant, whom the People may oppose; that Clergy-men are exempt from the Prince's Power, are none of his Subjects, and cannot be punish'd by him for any Crimes:* And having

* See it at large in *Hist. Jesuit.* p. 160. *Pro regulis indubitata habent quod ille excommunicandorum Regum potestatem habeat, quod Rex excommunicatus nihil sit aliud quam Tyrannus, cui Populus rebellare possit; --- quod omnes Regnicolæ qui minimum in Ecclesia ordinem habeant, si quodcunque crimen committant, illud pro læsæ Majestatis crimine haberi non possit, propterea quod Regum subditi non sint, nec ad eorum jurisdictionem pertineant,.*

enume-

Anno 1603.

enumerated several of their Treasons, they affirm, † *That it is absolutely necessary for them to renounce these Doctrines, or else France cannot with safety admit them to return.*

† *Oportet igitur ut illi qui tenent, & in regno vestro manere volunt, eas publicè in suis Collegiis abjurent.*

But though they were very desirous of Admission, they would not renounce those Positions for it; however by importunity, and the solicitation of the Pope, and others, they were at length received, but upon Conditions, ‖ *Two of which were, That they should build no Colleges without express Permission from the King; and that one of their number should be always near the King, to be accountable for the Actions of the Society.*

‖ *Hist. Jes. p. 494. Ne ulla Collegia ---sine expressa Regis permissione instituant.--- Ut semper aliquem habeant,* natione Gallum, qui Regi à Sacris concionibus esset, & de omnibus negotiis *rationem totius* Societatis nomine ipsi reddere possit.

Thus were they admitted, but marks of Distrust set upon them; though they have, by their Address, turn'd the latter of these Conditions, which was at first design'd for their Disgrace, into a mark of Honour, the King's Confessour being ever since a Jesuite.

Though the Gun-powder Plot was not ripe for Execution till two years after, yet they were consulting about it at this time; when after a long complaint of their Grievances, Mr. *Percy* told Mr. *Catesby*, that there was no way but to kill the King, and he was resolv'd to doe it: But that Gentleman desired him not to be so rash, for he had laid a surer Design, which would certainly effect it, without any danger to themselves; and then imparted to him the Contrivance of blowing up the King and Parliament.

Account of the Proceed. p. 164.

Hist. of the Gun-powder Plot. p. 5.	Which Design in *May*, the following year, the Conspiratours obliged themselves by Oath upon the Holy Sacrament to keep secret; † *Catesby* justifying the Action by the *Breves* which the Pope had sent to exclude King *James*; it being as lawfull to cast him out as to oppose his Entrance; and *Bates*, another of the Conspiratours, was assured by the Jesuite *Greenwell*, that the Cause and Action were good, and therefore it was his Duty to conceal it.	Anno 1604.
† Acct. of the Proceedings, p. 67.		
Ibid.	Upon the approaching of the Parliament they began to work, endeavouring to make a Mine under the Parliament-house; but soon after *Percy* hired a Cellar, in which they stowed the Gun-powder, with Billets heap'd upon it, to hide it in case of search.	
Fowl: Hist. p 513. An Account of the Proceed. p 168. † *Ib.* p. 58 59. Hist of the Gun-powder Treason p.17. *Wilson's* Hist. of K. *J.* p. 3'.	The *May* before the Plot was to be executed there was an Insurrection of the Romanists in *Wales*, but it was soon suppresst; yet all things went on in order to the fatal blow; when about a week before the Parliament was to sit, the Design was discovered, and so prevented; upon which the Conspiratours flew into † Rebellion, but were all either killed or taken by the Sheriff of *Worcestershire*	1605.
‖ Account of the Proceed. p. 6.	The ‖ King in his Speech to the Parliament soon after, told them that *Faux* confessed that they had no other cause moving them to the Design, but merely and only Religion; which was acknowledged by Sir *Everard Digby* at his Tryall, to be the chief Motive which enduced him to make one among them, and which he resolved to hazard his	
See his Papers at the end of the Account, p. 241, &c.	Life, his Estate, and all, to introduce; protesting, that if he had thought there had been the least sin in the Plot, he would not have been of it for all the World; and the Reason why he kept it secret, was because those who were best able to judge of the Lawfulness of it, had been acquainted with it, and given	

Anno 1605.

given way unto it; and therefore afterwards he calls it the best Cause.

The Persons, upon whose Authority he so much relied, were the Jesuites, who asserted the holiness of the Action; for *Garnet*, their Superiour, had affirmed that it was lawfull, and Father *Hammond* absolved them all after the Discovery, when they were in open Rebellion; and *Greenwell*, the Jesuite, rode about the Countrey to excite as many as he could to joyn with them; nay, † *Garnet* confessed that *Catesby* in his name did satisfie the rest of the Lawfulness of the Fact. * *Parsons* had kept a Correspondency with that Jesuite to promote it, and at the same time (not willing to discover it to them, and yet desirous of their Prayers,) ‖ ordered the Students of his College at *Rome* to pray for the Intention of their Father Rectour: And after the Discovery, * Father *Hall*, encouraged some of the Traitors, who began to doubt that the Action was unlawfull, seeing God had defeated it in so providential a manner, telling them, that we must not judge of the Cause by the Event; that this was no more than what happened to the Eleven Tribes when they went up at first to fight against *Benjamin*, and that the Christians were often defeated by the Turks; nay, so highly was it approv'd by that Order, that, not to mention here the Honours done to the Conspiratours, since their Deaths, several Jesuites gloried in, and bragg'd of it; for a little before the Discovery, Father *Flood* caused the Jesuites at *Lisbon* to spend a great deal of Money in Powder, on a Festival day, to try the force of it, and persuaded one *John How*, a Merchant, and other Catholicks, to go over into *England*, and expect their Redemption there: And Father *Thompson* was wont afterwards to boast to his Scholars at *Rome*, how oft his Shirt

Account of the Proceedings, p. 105, 172.

† *Causab. Ep. ad Front. Ducæum*, p. 99. *Lond.*1611.4to.
* Account of the Proceed. p. 175.
‖ *Fow.* p. 509.

* Account of the Proceed. p. 172.

† *Robins. Anat.* of the English Nunnery at Lisbon, p. 8. *Lond.*1630.4to.

Fow. p. 510.

was

was wetted with digging under the Parliament House.

Anno 1605.

Fowlis, p. 509.
And that the Pope himself was concerned in the Design is more than probable, for it is confessed by a Jesuite that there were three Bulls granted by him, which should have been published if the Conspiracy had succeeded; and Sir *Everard Digby* hath left it under his hand, that it was not the Pope's mind that any Stirs should be hindered which were undertaken for the Catholick Cause.

In his Papers ubi supr. p. 250.

The Pope's carriage after the Discovery is another shrewd Argument that he was privy to the Plot, for he not only made no Declaration either by Word or Writing in abhorrence of it, but when * *Greenway*, one of the Conspirators, escaped to *Rome*, he advanced him to the Dignity of Penitentiary, and † *Gerard*, another, was a Confessour at St. *Peters* in the same City.

* Copley's Reasons, p. 22.
* Vindication of the History of Gunp. Tr. p. 74.

This execrable Conspiracy appeared so horrid and unworthy, not only of religious Men, but contrary to humane Nature, that † sixteen of the Students under the Jesuites at *Rome*, forsook the College, and some of them renounced the Roman Church; and * Mr. *Copley*, who had been a Priest some years, (as appears by his Reasons, one of sound Learning and judgment,) assures us, that it was one of the Causes of his Conversion.

† Fowl. p. 509.
*Copley's Reas. p. 21.

Yet were there many found among the Romanists who justified the Design, hardly any condemning it: Thus the same Gentleman professes, that though some termed it an inconsiderate Act, yet he could never meet with any one Jesuite who blamed it. The * Conspiratours justified themselves, and even at their deaths would acknowledge no fault: And when † *Faux* and *Winter* were admitted to discourse together in the Tower, they affirmed

Ib. p. 23.

* K. James Premon p. 231. of his works.
† Account of Proceedings, p. 125.

Anno 1605.

med, they were sorry that no body set forth a Defence or Apology for the Action; but yet they would maintain the Cause at their Deaths; nay there was one who had the hardiness to attempt * to justifie the Design from the imputation of Cruelty, because both Seeds and Root of an evil Herb must be destroyed; And when some of the Plotters escaped to *Callis*, the Governour assured them of the King's Favour, and that though they lost their Country they should be received there; they replyed, That the loss of their Country was the least part of their Grief; but their sorrow was that they could not bring so brave a Design to perfection.

And notwithstanding *Garnet* was so deep in the Conspiracy, yet † Mr. *Wilson* placed him among the Martyrs, in his English Martyrology; and it is affirmed by * one who liv'd among them, that he and *Campion* are beatified by the Pope, which is the next degree to Canonization, and that every one of them is painted in the Jesuites Churches, with the Title of Blessed Father; † and we are assured that *Garnet*'s Picture was set up in their Church at *Rome*, among their Martyrs, several years after; and * St. *Amour*, a Doctour of *Sorbon*, found his Pictures commonly sold at *Rome*, in the year 1651. with this Inscription, Father Henry Garnet, *hang'd and quarter'd at* London, *for the Catholick Faith*; by which they shew themselves either Approvers of the Design, to that degree as to count it a point of their Faith, or else they must appear Deceivers of the People, and Slanderers of the English Nation, in affirming, that he dyed for his Religion, when he justly suffered for the most hellish Conspiracy

* See Key for Cathol. p. 434

Hist. of the Gun-powder Treas. p. 29.

† Copley's Reasons, p. 22.

* Robins. Anat. p. 3.

† *Primarius quidem Baro Scotus, idemque spectatissimæ in Religione constantiæ, cum Romam venisset, in Templo illo Jesuitarum, inter alios sodalitatis illius Martyres, Henrici Garnetti effigiem vidit. Bernard. Giral. Paravi. pro Repub. Ven. Apolog. p. 107.*

* St. Amour's Journal. p. 58. Lond. 1664.
Fol. ----- Pater Henricus Garnettus Anglus, Londini pro Fide Catholica suspensus, & sectus. 2. Maii. 1606.

that

that was ever laid; yet *Delrio*, and *Gordon*, two Jefuites, went farther; the firft in Profecution of his Determination in the point which we mentioned before, compares him to *Dionyfius*, the *Areopagite*; the latter placing him in Heaven, defires him to intercede there for the converfion of *England*, and it was once publickly prayed in *Louvain*, *O holy Henry! Intercede for us.*

Anno 1605.

Cowl. p. 520.

But they had defigns elfewhere at the fame time that this their holy Martyr was promoting their Caufe in *England*; King *Henry* of *France* his Life was fo burthenfome to the Jefuites, that they were impatient, fo that Father *Coton*, the King's Confeffour, or rather Hoftage for his Society, to be fatisfied in the point, wrote down feveral queftions which he had propounded to a Maid faid to be poffeffed, one of which was how long the King fhould live; which is a capital Crime in itfelf; * *For* (as *Tertullian* long fince argued) *who hath any bufinefs to make fuch an Enquiry, except he hath defigns againft his Prince, or hath fome hopes of advancement by his death.*

Vindic. of the Sincer. of the Prot. Relig p. 132. out of *Thuanus ad an.* 1604.
* *Tertul. Apol. c.* 35.
Cui autem opus eſt ſcrutari ſuper Cæſaris ſalute, niſi à quo adverſus illum aliquid cogitatur, aut poſt illam ſperatur, & ſuſtinetur.

And as bufie was the Pope *Paul* the Fifth for the advancement of the Roman Caufe, he fell out with the Duke of * *Savoy* this Year, for prefenting an Abbey to Cardinal *Pio*; and to fhew his Authority over Princes and States, (which is a kind of depofing them, and clear Evidence of Popifh Principles,) when the Commonwealth of *Luca* made an Edict againft the Proteftants, though he liked the thing, yet he pretended they had no power in thofe matters, and therefore commanded them to raze the Edict out of their Records, and he would publifh one for the fame purpofe by his own Authority; and

*Fowl. p. 455.

Idem. p. 456.

Anno 1605. and when the State of *Genoa* prohibited some seditious Meetings of Ecclesiasticks, he threatened them with Excommunication, and forced them to recall their Order.

But the *Venetians* would not be frighted by his Thunders, though he threatened them with the same Censure, if they did not speedily revoke their Decrees concerning the building of Churches, and giving Lands to the Church, (which they had prohibited any to doe without the Senate's Order,) and required them to deliver two Clergymen, whom they had imprisoned for many horrid Crimes; concluding his *Breve* with an Assertion of his Power to deprive Kings, and that he had Legions of Angels for this Assistance.

Fowl. Hist. 455, &c. Histor. Jes. p. 306.

1606. But when the Senate would not gratifie him in thus yielding their Rights to an Usurper, the Pope told their Ambassadour, that the Exemption of Clergy-men from the Jurisdiction of the Magistrate was *Jure divino*, that his Cause was the Cause of God, and he would be obeyed; and therefore in a Consistory of one and forty Cardinals he published a Bull of Excommunication against that State, wherein he declares, * *That by the Authority of Almighty God, and the Apostles* Peter *and* Paul, *the Duke and Senate of* Venice, *if within four and twenty days after the publication of the Bull they do not revoke their Decrees, are excommunicated; and if they continue obstinate three days more, he lays an Interdict upon the whole State, forbidding the Clergy to perform Divine Offices in any part of their Dominions, and threatens far-*

Fowl. p 458.

* *Authoritate omnipotentii Dei, ac B. Petri & Pauli Apostolorum ejus, ac nostra, nisi Dux & Senatus intra viginti quatuor dies a die publicationis præsentium --- computandos prædicta Decreta omnia, &c. revocaverint, &c. --- excommunicamus, & excommunicatos nunciamus & declaramus. Et si dicti Dux & Senatus per tres dies post lapsum dictorum viginti quatuor dierum, excommunicationis sententiam animo sustinuerint indurato, --- universum temporale Dominium dict. Reip. ecclesiastico Interdicto supponimus, --- iliisque etiam Pænas contra ipsos --- juxta sacrorum Canonum dispositionem --- declarandi facultatem reservamus. --- Dat. Apr. 18. Anno 1606.*

farther *Punishments*, according to the sacred Canons.

This Bull he expected would gain his point, by causing the Ecclesiasticks to withdraw themselves, and that the People, seeing themselves deprived of Church-Offices, would run into Sedition; but the Event answered not his Expectation, for the People joined unanimously with the Senate; but the Jesuites, and others, refused to celebrate Mass, upon which they were banished the Dominions of *Venice*; after † which they did all they could to stir up the Common People: But not succeeding in this, the Pope published a Jubilee, granting Indulgence to all but those of Interdicted places; this he expected would make the People murmur, but he was deceived in that point too; so that he declared in a full Consistory that he would have War with the State of *Venice*, and called the Spaniards to his aid; but finding the Senate resolute in Defence of their Rights, he was glad to recall his Bull, and make a Peace with them, and though he earnestly pressed for the Restauration of the Jesuites, yet he could not obtain it.

About this time the Oath of Allegiance being established by Law, the Romanists sent to *Rome* to know what they should doe in this Case, where it was consulted by seven or eight of their learnedest Divines, who all agreed, that the Pope's Power of chastizing Princes is a Point of Faith, and consequently cannot be denied without denying of the Faith; and the Pope told Father *Parsons*, and *Fitzherbert*, he could not hold those for Catholicks who took the Oath; which he soon after declared by his Breve, addressed to the Romanists of *England*, Septemb. 22. 1606. wherein he affirms, † *That they cannot, without most evident and grievous wronging of*

† *Fowlis* Hist. l. 453, &c.

Ib. p. 525, 527.

† *Non potes is absque evidentissima gravissi-*

Anno 1606.

Anno 1606. of *God's Honour, bind themselves by the Oath, seeing it contains many things contrary to Faith and Salvation.*

mique divini honoris injuriâ obligare vos juramento, —— cùm multa contineat quæ fidei & saluti apertè aversantur.

1607. But when some Romanists who had taken it began to question the *Breve*, willing to think it was obtained from his Holiness by surreption; he sent † another to undeceive them, wherein he blames them for entertaining such thoughts, and assures them, *That it was written upon mature deliberation, and therefore they are bound fully to observe it, rejecting all interpretation to the contrary*; upon which several who were willing before refused it, some of whom were imprisoned.

*Aug.23.1607.

Decrevimus vobis significare Literas illas post longam & gravem de omnibus quæ in illis continentur deliberationem adhibitam fuisse scriptas; & eb id teneri vos illas omnino observare, omni interpretatione secùs suadente rejectâ.

It is an hard thing for men accustomed to doe evil to learn to doe well, which Truth *Tyr-Oen* is a great Example of, for notwithstanding after his frequent Rebellions he was pardoned by King *James*, and received into favour, yet returning into *Ireland* he began new Contrivances, and fearing he was discovered, fled this year into *Flanders*, which caused the King to publish a severe Proclamation against him; from thence he went to *Rome*, where he was maintained at the Pope's charge till his death.

Fowlis's Hist. p. 495.

This same Year *Parsons* published his Treatise tending to Mitigation, wherein he labours to take off the imputation of rebellious Principles from the Romanists, and yet he tells us in the same Book, " That this is Catholick Doctrine, that in publick " Perils of the Church, and Common-Wealth, " Christ our Saviour hath not left us wholly re-" medilesss, but besides the natural Right which " each Kingdom hath to defend themselves, in cer-

Treatise of Mitigation, p. 176.

" tain cafes, he left alfo fupreme Power in his High
" Prieft, and immediate Subftitute, to direct and
" moderate that Power, and to add alfo of his own
" when extraordinary Need requireth, though with
" great deliberation. Where we have a plain jufti-
fication of the Pope and People's Power to depofe
and refift their Princes, a moft excellent Argument
to clear the Papifts of Difloyalty.

Hift. Jefuit.
p. 332.

Hift. Jef.
p. 251.
Vindicat. of
Prot. Relig.
p. 1133.

Though we find no Plots difcovered this year in
England, yet in *Tranfilvania* the Jefuites were employed in poifoning *Stephen Potfcay* the Prince: And
in *France* Father *Cotton* recommended a Spaniard to
the King, who had not been in the Court many
hours, when the King had Intelligence of his coming
from *Barcellona* purpofely to poifon him; upon this
he fent for Father *Coton*, who defired his Majefty
not to give any Credit to the advice; and when the
King ordered him to produce the Spaniard, he pretended to feek him, but at his return told his Majefty that he was efcaped, and he could not find
him.

Fowl. p. 529
530, 531.

Si intra tempus
hoc facere diftu-
lerint, eos fa-
cultatibus &
privilegiis om-
nibus--prives.

This year the Pope fent another *Breve* into *England*,
directed to the Arch-Prieft, *forbidding him to take the*
Oath, and commanding him to deprive all Priefts of
their Faculties who took it, except they immediately re-
nounc'd it; prohibiting likewife the refort of any to
the Proteftant Churches.

At the fame time Divines of *Italy*, *Germany*, and
France, wrote againft it, all grounding their Excep-
tions upon this, that it takes away the Pope's Power
of Depofing Kings.

Hiftor. Jefuit.
p. 297.

Idem, p. 226,
227, 228.

So rebellious had the Writings and Practices of
the Jefuites been, that the *Bohemians* petition'd the
Emperour againft them; and the *Valefian* Magi-
ftrates refufed to admit them, becaufe wherever
they came they difturbed the publick Peace, and
were

Anno 1610.

were under such a tie of blind Obedience, that if their Superiour enjoin'd them a treasonable Attempt they must obey.

They had made it their Business, for some time, to endeavour to get footing in *Transilvania*, but when all their Importunity could not prevail, they engaged several of the Nobility in a Design against the Prince's Life, which proceeded so far that one of the Conspiratours attempted to run him through, but was prevented, and several of his Companions taken, the rest escaped. Hist. Jesuit. p. 332, 333. Vindic. of the Sincer. of the Plot. Relig. p. 135.

And now King *Henry* the Great of *France* having amassed a very considerable Treasure, prepared for some great Design, which the Romanists grew so jealous of, that they secretly caused several to subscribe their Obedience to the Pope, in a Book which was kept on purpose; it was half written through, and some names subscribed in bloud; several Designs were formed against his Life, four *Piedmontiers*, a *Lorrainer*, and three others, conspired his Death; advice was given of several other Plots from many other places, and Reports were spread in foreign parts that he was killed: ☞Father *Hardy*, in his Sermon at St. *Severius* in *Paris*, reflecting upon the King's Treasure, said, *That Kings heaped up Treasures to make themselves feared, but there needed but a blow to kill a King*. All these were but Fore-runners of that horrid Murther which was committed in a few Weeks after by *Ravilliac*, once a Monk, who stabbed him to the Heart with a poisoned Knife, as he was going to the Arsenal in his Coach, so that he expired in an instant; upon his Examination he confessed that he resolved to murther the King, who he supposed had a Design to make War upon the Pope, be- For. p 471. Ib. p. 470, &c. Hist. Jesuit. p. 261. *Hic quidem mos est Regum, ut ingentes Thesauros ad sui amplitudinem & aliorum terrorem colligant, at rusticulum unum ad Regem supprimendum sufficere.* Histor. Jesuit. p. 260, 261. Fowlis's Hist. p. 471, 472.

cause

cause making War against his Holiness is the same | Anno 1610.
as to make War against God, seeing the Pope was
God, and God was the Pope; and that he had revealed his Design to the Jesuite *d'Aubigny* in Confession, and shewed him the Knife, and that he had heard several of that Order maintain the Lawfulness of it in their Sermons.

Histor. Jesuit. p. 219, &c.

No sooner was the King dead, but the Jesuites | 1611.
desired leave to teach Schools in their Colleges; which acquest the Parliament took into consideration, and required that they should first declare, That it is unlawfull for any Person to conspire the death of the King; that no Ecclesiastick hath any Power over the Temporal Rights of Princes; and that all are to render the same Obedience to their Governours, which Christ gave to *Cæsar*. These Positions were proposed to them to subscribe, but they refused to doe it without leave from their General; upon which they were prohibited by a Decree of Parliament to teach, and threatened with a farther Deprivation if they would not obey.

Fowl. p. 343.

The Romanists had tried all manner of ways to | 1613.
deprive King *James* of his Life or Crown, but finding none successfull, they had the Impudence to publish a Book this year, affirming, that His Majesty was a counterfeit, and not the Son of Queen *Mary* of *Scotland*.

The Year following Cardinal *Perron*, who had | 1614.
been one of the young Cardinal of *Bourbon*'s Party against King *Henry* the Fourth, in the Assembly of Estates in *France*, asserted not only that Subjects may be absolved from their Allegiance, and Princes deposed in case of Heresie, but that they who hold the contrary are Schismaticks and Hereticks. This Speech was made to divert the Estates from imposing an Oath like our Oath of Allegiance; which

See his Speech at large in his *Diverses Oeuvres, Paris, 1633. fol.*

Design

Anno 1614. Design so disturbed the ‖ Pope, that he affirmed the Voters of it were Enemies to the common Good, and mortal Adversaries to the Chair of *Rome*.

‖ *Forv.* p 52.

And about the same time *Suarez* printed his Book at *Colen*, wherein he teaches, that Kings may be put to Death by their own Subjects; which Treatise came into the World with the Approbation of the Bishop of *Conimbria*, of *Silvis*, and *Lamego*, and the University of *Alcalum*, with several others.

His *Defens. Fi. dei Catholicæ.* See *Brutum Fulmen*, p. 205, &c.

In *Scotland* one Father *Ogelby*, a Jesuite, was taken, who being asked whether the Pope be Judge in Spirituals over His Majesty, refused to answer, except the question were put to him by the Pope's Authority; but affirmed that the Pope might excommunicate the King; at his Trial he protested against the Judges, that he could not own them, for the K. had no Authority but what was derivative from his Predecessours, who acknowledged the Pope's jurisdiction; adding, *If the King will be to me as they were to mine, he shall be my King, otherwise I value him not:* And as for that Question, *Whether the K. deposed by the Pope, may be lawfully killed, Doctours of the Church hold the affirmative not improbably, and I will not say it is unlawfull to save my Life.*

Frankl. Annal. p. 6, 7.

In *France* several of the Princes raised Commotions, which were appeased with conferring places of Trust and Honour upon the chief among them, who were headed by the Prince of *Conde*; Fruits (as the Historian observes) accustomed to be reaped in *France*, from that which in other places is punished by the Executioner.

Nani's History of *Venice*, p. 33, 34.

1615. Not satisfied with their Honours, they took arms again under the same Leader, and passed the *Loire*; but the Prince of *Conde* falling sick. Matters were composed by the Endeavours of the English Ambassadour, and some others.

Ib. p. 58, 59.

(74)

Nani's History of Venice, p. 65, 99.

  In *Savoy* Conspiracies were formed against that Duke's Life, and to deliver up the Prince, his Son, to the Spaniards, but timely discovery prevented them, and preserved the Duke from another Design of some who undertook to poison him.

Hist. Jesuit. p. 297, 299.

  The next Year the Jesuites were banished *Bohemia*, and *Moravia*, for coining Money, and sowing Dissentions between the Magistrates and People,

*Nani, p. 121, 122.

and a Plot was discovered at * *Venice*, against the Senatours, whom the Conspiratours designed to murther, by a sudden Insurrection, (assisted by the Marquess of *Bedmar*, Ambassadour from *Spain*, and the Duke of *Ossuna*, Viceroy of *Naples*,) and make

* Consp. of the Span. agt. the State of Venice, p. 15, 16. Lon. 1675. 8vo.

an utter subversion of the State; * this was carried on, in conjunction with the Spaniards, by those Citizens, and others, who were the Pope's Partisans, and a number of Factious Persons, discontented with the Actions of the Senate, who longed for a change, and would stick at nothing to effect it. And in

† Nani p. 124.

France the † Queen Mother being imprisoned, the Duke *D'Espernon*, with a strong Party, rebelled in her Defence; but before the King's Army was come up against him, he procured his Pardon, and the Liberty of the Queen.

  Soon after this the Jesuites were driven out of

‖ Hist. Jesuit. p. 300, 301. * Nani, p. 151. † Id. p. 159.

‖ *Hungary*, and *Silesia*, for their seditious Practices; and * another Rebellion broke out in *France*, which the King marched in Person to suppress: † In the *Valteline* the Revolt was universal, the Governours of Provinces, and the Heads of Families, were all murthered, and under pretence of defending the Roman Catholick Religion, all manner of outrages were committed, and a new form of Government erected; these Broils continued some time, and the bitterness of the Papists was such, that they would make no accommodation, if the Protestants were

tole-

Anno		
1620.	tolerated there; * so that if a Protestant Bailiff be sent among them, he cannot publickly exercise his Religion.	* Burnet's Trav. p. 81
1622.	At this time the Match between Prince *Charles* and the *Infanta* was prosecuted, at least with a seeming willingness on both sides, and being to have some Romish Priests of her Houshold, the Pope urged very earnestly that they might be exempt from His Majesty's jurisdiction, so very diligent he was in catching at any shadow which might seem to favour the Exemption of the Clergy.	Wilson's Hist. of Great Brit. p. 203.
1625.	Three Years after this *Sanctarellus* his Book was printed at *Rome*, wherein the Deposing Power was asserted in its utmost latitude, and though Father *Coto*, and two other Jesuites, were required to answer it, yet no reply appeared; the former affirming before the Parliament, that though he disapproved the Doctrine in *France*, yet he would assent to it if he were at *Rome*.	Fowlis, p. 476. Mister. Pret. 60, 61. Sen. Quid si essetis Romæ? P. Coto. Mutaretur nobiscum cœlo animus, sentiremus ut Romæ.
1626.	The Oath of Allegiance being vigorously press'd in *England*, the Pope sent a Bull to the Romanists, exhorting them to continue firm, * and *let their Tongue rather cleave to the Roof of their Mouth then permit the Authority of St. Peter, to be diminished by that Oath*; and commanding them strictly to observe the *Breves* of Pope *Paul* the Fifth; and † Father *Fisher* justified *Suarez*, and the Doctrine of his Book, asking, what could be found prejudicial in it to Princely Authority; and affirming that if it contained any such thing it would not be permitted in Catholick Kingdoms.	* See Baiting of the Pope's Bull, in init.— ad hæreat lingua vestra faucibus vestris, priusquam authoritatem B. Petri eâ jurisjurandi formulâ imminutam detis. † Jesuits Reasons unreasonable, p. 116.
1627.	We have mention'd that the exemption of the Clergy was desired by the Pope in the Treaty for the	Rushworth's Collect. part. 1. p. 427.

the Spanish Match; and now his Emissaries in this Nation affirmed that the King could have nothing to doe with her Majesties Chaplains, because he was an Heretick; and his Holiness threatned to declare those to be Apostates who should seek their Establishment in the Queens Family from the King. *Anno 1627.*

But though these were plain Indications of what they desired, yet they kept their Designs so secret, that they were not discovered till some time after; but there was a Conspiracy detected at *Genoa*, which, if it had not been prevented, would have ended in the Murther of the Nobility, and Alteration of the Government. *1628.*

Nani's History of Venice, p. 283.

And the next Year a Plot was detected in *Mantua* against the Life of the Prince, and some Officers apprehended, who would have betray'd *Viadana* to the Governour of *Millan*. *1629.*

Idem. p. 312.

In *Ireland* the Papists assaulted the Archbishop of *Dublin*, wounded several of his Followers, and forced him to fly for his Life; following him in a tumultuous manner along the streets; and that they had several seditious Designs in hand at the same time, is evident from the Confession of † *MacEnerry*, a Dominican, who for this very reason left the Church of *Rome*, because of her rebellious Doctrines, and the many Conspiracies he had taken an Oath of Secresie to conceal, which he observed inviolably; and though he informed the Bishop of *Limrick*, that there were many Plots then contriving against his Majesty's Government, yet for his Oaths sake he would not name any Persons who were concerned in them. *1620.*

Foxes & Firebrands, pt. 2. p. 72, 73.

† *Hunting of the Rom. Fox, p. 216, 217.*

The Duke of *Orleance* had retired in disgust from Court some years since, and was received by the Duke of *Lorrain*; but being forced this year to leave that retreat, he went to *Brussells*, from whence, aided *1632.*

Nani's History of Venice, p. 310, &c.

Anno	aided by the Spaniards, he marched at the head of an Army into *France*, but was defeated, and several of his Adherents executed.
1633.	While *France* was thus almost continually pestered with Rebellions, the Designs of the Papists ripened apace in *Ireland*, ; they had erected Friaries, in the Countrey instead of those which were dissolved in *Dublin*; and even in that City they had a College of Students, whereof Father *Paul Harris* was Dean, and at a Synodical meeting of their Clergy, they decreed, that it was not lawfull to take the Oath of Allegiance.
1640.	If it were not that all the Designs of that Party from the Year 1630. to 1640. were summed up, and perfected in the Rebellion in *Ireland*, and the execrable Civil Wars of *England*, I should wonder how they came to be so still, and that no more Conspiracies were discovered, besides that great one which *Andreas ab Habernsfield* was informed of in *Holland*, and of which he sent the King an Account, under the hand of the Discoverer, who affirms, that one *Maxfield* was sent into *Scotland*, to stir up a Rebellion there, and that the King was to be poisoned; for which end they kept a strong Poison in an Indian Nut, which he had often seen: They had likewise another Design, if they could prevail upon the Scots, or discontented English, to rebell, that thereby the King should be straitened, and forced to depend on the Papists for assistance, and then they would make their own Terms, and secure to themselves a publick Liberty, which if he refused to consent to, they would not only desert him, but dispatch him with the Indian Nut, which they reserved on purpose.

Bp B:h:?.

Long's History of Plots, p.100.

See whole Account published under this Title, The Designs of the Papists, *Lond*. 1678. 4to.

He gives also an Account of the Persons concerned in the Plot, among whom were several Ladies of Quality, for whose Encouragement the Pope sent
a *Breve*

Anno 1640.

<small>See it in Frankland's Annals, p. 865, 866.</small>

a *Breve* to Sir *Toby Mathews*, one of the principal Conspiratours, wherein he exhorts him, and the Women engaged with him, to proceed with diligence in the Design; assuring them, *That he did not despair to see the Authority of the Holy See (which was subverted in* England *by a Woman) again restored in a very little time, by the Endeavours of those Heroick Ladies.*

<small>*Non diffidimus,---- quia sicut occasione unius Fœminæ Authoritas Sedis Apostolicæ in Regno Angliæ suppressa fuit, sic nunc per tot Heroicas Fœminas,--- brevi modò restituenda sit.*</small>

1641.

This *Breve* is an unanswerable Evidence that the succeeding Troubles derived their original from the insatiate Lust of Rule which possessed the Pope, who herein approves of those very Methods which afterwards proved the Ruine of that excellent Prince, and so miserably distracted these poor Nations.

<small>See the History of the Irish Rebellion, fol.</small>

But he appeared more publickly an Abbettor of the Irish Massacre and Rebellion, wherein so many thousand Protestants were murthered in cold bloud, sending his Nuncio to assist, and affording them all the aid that he was able to give; a Design laid with so much secresie, and executed with so much cruelty, that nothing but the very Spirit of Popery could be barbarous enough to engage in it; in prosecution of which they did all they could totally to beat the English out of the Kingdom.

<small>Nani's Hist. p. 493.</small>

The same year the Marquess de *Villa Real*, the Duke *de Camina*, and the Marquess *d'Armamar*, who by the Instigation of the Archbishop of *Braga*, had undertaken to kill the King of *Portugal*, Father to Her Majesty the Queen Dowager of *England*, and to fire the Ships and the City in several places, that they might have the better opportunity to promote the Interest of the Spaniards, were put to death.

Nor

(79)

Anno 1641.	Nor did *France* yet enjoy any more quiet, where the Count *de Soiffons*, and the Duke of *Guife*, and others, raifed a Rebellion, and routed the King's Army, but the Count being flain with his own Piftol, the Confederacy was foon broken.	*Nani's* Hift. p. 495, &c.
1642.	Yet the very next Year the Duke of *Orleance* combined with the Spaniards, who were to affift him with Forces for a new Rebellion.	*Id.* P. 535.
	The Pope had involved *Ireland* in Bloud the former year, and in this the Wars began in *England*, where feveral † Priefts were found among the dead at *Edghill* Battle; but the Endeavours of his Holinefs to encreafe thofe miferable Confufions, were managed with all imaginable Secrefie, while the Irifh were openly commended by him, and * affured of his Prayers for their fuccefs in his *Breve* to *Owen O Neal*, dated *Octob.* 8. 1642. and fo willing was he to lay hold on all occafions for the exercifing his Depofing Power, that becaufe the † Prince of *Parma* offended him, he declared him to have incurred the greater Excommunication, and deprived him of all his Dominions and Dignities.	† *Long's* Hift. of Plots, p. 64. * *Nos divinam Clementiam indefinenter orantes, ut adverfariorum conatus in nihilum redigat, &c.* See it at large in the Append. to the Hift. of the Irifh Rebel. p. 59. † *Nani's* Hift. p. 515.
1643. 1644. 1645.	But not content with fending the forementioned *Breve* to *O Neal*, his Holinefs granted a Bull of plenary Indulgence, *May* 25. 1643. to all the Catholicks in *Ireland*, who joined in the Rebellion; which was profecuted as fiercely as the Pope could defire, and a defence of it fet forth by an † Irifh Jefuite in *Portugal* (though the Title-page mentions *Franckfort*,) who afferts, *That the Englifh Kings have no Title or Right to* Ireland; *that if they had, yet it is the Duty of the Irifh to deprive them of their Rights, feeing*	Hift. of the Irifh Remon. Pref. p. † *Difputatio Apolog. de jure Reg. Hibern. pro Cath. Hibern. adverf. Heret. Anglos,* p 65. cited by *Walfh* in the Hiftory of the Irifh Remonftrance, p. 735, 737. in thefe words: *Ordinis Regni optimo jure poterant ac debebant omni do-*

they.

they are declared Hereticks, and Tyrants; that this Power of depoſing ſuch Princes is inherent in every State; but if the Authority of the Holy See be added to that Power, none but a Fool, or an Heretick, will deny what the Doctours of Divinity, and of the Civil and Canon Law, do generally teach, and which is confirmed by Reaſons and Examples.

<small>minio Hiberniæ privatæ tales Reges, poſtquam facti ſunt Haretici atque Tyranni —— Hoc enim jus & poteſtas in omni Regno & Republica eſt. —— Jam ſi conſenſui Regni in hac re accederet Authoritas Apoſtolica, quis niſi Hæreticus, vel Stultus audebit negare quod hic affirmamus, & Doctores Theologi, & Juris utriuſq́ue periti paſſim docent, rationes probant, exempla ſuadent.</small>

Anno 1607.

And ſo far did the Pope approve of the Contents of this Book, that when, ſoon after its publication, the Iriſh had ſubmitted to the King, and promiſed to aſſiſt him in his Wars, His Holineſs by his Nuncio took upon him to be their General, abſolved them from their Oaths, and impriſoned and threatened the Lives of thoſe who had promoted the peace, and deſired to return to the King's Subjection, which renewed the Rebellion again, and brought infinite Miſeries on that bigotted Nation.

<small>Ld. Clarendon againſt Creſſy, p. 246.</small>

At the ſame time above * an hundred of the Romiſh Clergy were ſent into *England* by Order from *Rome*, who, the better to promote the Diviſions there, were inſtructed in ſeveral Trades, both handicraft and others; theſe, upon their arrival, were ordered to diſperſe themſelves, and give Intelligence every month to their Superiours abroad; accordingly they liſted themſelves in the Parliament Army, and kept a conſtant correſpondence with their Brethren, who for the ſame end ſerved under the King.

<small>* Bp. Bramhall's Letters to A. P. Uſher, ap. Uſher's Life & Letters, p. 611.</small>

1609.

The next year many of theſe Miſſioners were in conſultation with thoſe in the King's Army, to whom they ſhewed their Bulls, and Licenſes, for taking part with the Parliament about the beſt methods

<small>Id. p. 612.</small>

Anno 1647.

thods to advance their Cause; and having concluded that there was no way so effectual as to dispatch the King, some were sent to *Paris*, to consult the Faculty of *Sorbonne* about it, who return'd this Answer, That it is lawfull for Roman Catholicks to work Changes in Governments, for the Mother Church's advancement, and chiefly in an Heretical Kingdom, and so they might lawfully make away the King; * which Sentence was confirmed to the same Persons by the Pope, and his Council, upon their going to *Rome* to have his Holiness's Resolution in the Point.

* Vindic. of the sincerity of the Prot. Relig. p. 59.

And now those of them who had before followed the King after his flight from *Oxford*, * agreed to desert the Royal Cause; and, as one of them inform us, to ingratiate themselves with the Enemy, by acting some notorious piece of Treachery; and Father *Carr*, who went by the name of Quarter-Master *Laurence*, declared, that he could with a safer Conscience join with and fight for the Roundheads than the Cavaliers; in prosecution of which Resolve they dispersed themselves into all the Garisons of the King's Party, to endeavour the Revolt of the Soldiers to the Parliament; in which they succeeded as they had projected, my Authour being one of those who seduced the *Wallingford* Horse from their Obedience; and in *Scotland* the Lord *Sinclare*, a pretended Presbyterian, but a real Papist, commanded a Regiment of his own Religion, and it being a Maxim receiv'd among them, *That the surest way to promote the Catholick Cause was to weaken the Royal Party, and advance the other*, they bent all their Endeavours to expedite and accelerate the King's Death; and His Majesty having in the Treaty of the Isle of *Wight* consented to pass five strict Bills against Popery, the Jesuites in *France*, at a general

* *Mutatus Polemo.* p. 4, 5.

Id. p. 6. 18. 26. 32.

Vindic. of the sincer. of the Prot. Relig. p. 65.

M.

ral meeting there, presently resolved to take off his Head; and this His Majesty had notice of by an Express from thence, but two days before his removal from the Isle of *Wight*.

Cressey's Exomolog. p. 72. Paris, 1647. 8vo.

This Year Mr. *Cressy* published the Reasons of his leaving the Church of *England*, and turning Romanist, wherein obviating the Objection so often made against the Romanists about their rebellious Principles and Practices, he sets down a Declaration, which he affirms that they were all ready to subscribe, and which differs but little from our Oath of Allegiance: But here we may see what Credit can be given to the representations of their Doctrines, which their Writers study to make as favourable as possible: For though Mr. *Cressy* thought himself a good Representer in this point, yet his Superiours were of another mind; and therefore that Edition was soon bought up, and in the next the Profession

Ld. Clarendon against Cressey. p. 76, 77.

of Obedience quite left out; and that this was not an omission of the Printer, but the action of his Superiours, we are assured by an honourable Person from Mr. *Cressy*'s own mouth, and we shall find in a little time, that the same form hath been condembed by the Pope himself.

But the ensuing year, as it was dolefull to the English Nation, so it brought great disturbances to the most potent Princes of *Europe*; in *France* the

Priorato's Hist. of France, p. 11, &c. Lond. 1676. fol.

Parisians rose in Arms, shot at the Lord Chancellour *Sequier*, and wounded his Daughter, barricadoed the Streets, and forced the King to set the Counsellour *Broussell*, and other factious Persons, at Liberty.

And at the Treaty at *Osnebrugh*, when by several Articles of the Peace the possession of Church Lands were assured to the Protestant Princes; the Pope displeased with it, took upon him to make void the

Anno 1647.

1648.

Anno 1648.

the Peace by a * special Bull, declaring all those Articles unjust, and of no Force, and commanding the Princes concerned to observe his Bull; in which he renews his Claim to the superiority over Princes, and particularly the Emperour, not only by the Bull in general, but by asserting, that || *the Electours of the Empire were established by the Authority of the Bishop of Rome.*

* *Declarat: SS. Dom. nost: Innoc. divinâ Providentiâ Pæ 10. nullit: tis articuloru nuperæ pacis Germaniæ, Religioni Cathol cæ, Sedi Apostolicæ, & qu: modo libet pre*

judicialium,—— See it in *Hoornbeck Disputat. ad Bull. Inn.* 10. † *Numerus septem Electoru Imperii*—— *Apostolicâ Authoritate præfinitus.*——

But to come to their Contrivances in *England*; where, when several Papists had subscribed to some Propositions, importing the unlawfulness of murthering Princes, and breaking Faith with Hereticks; and that the Pope hath no power to absolve Subjects from their Allegiance; the very same with the Declaration published the year before by Mr. *Cressy*, this Action was condemned at *Rome*, where by a Congregation it was decreed unlawfull.

H st of the Irish Remon. p. 523, 524.

And now in prosecution of the Pope and *Sorbon*'s Sentence the last year, that excellent Prince, King *Charles* the Martyr, was by their contrivances brought to the Block; which though they were willing to disown now, yet at that time they were very sollicitous to let the World know that they were the promoters of it; * the Friars of *Dunkirk* expressed great resentment that the Jesuites would engross to themselves the Glory of that Work, whereas they had laboured as diligently and successfully as any, and in several other places the Friars were very jealous, left that Order should rob them of their part of the Honour: And the Benedictines were not a little carefull to secure their Land in *England* from the Jesuites, for they thought their return sure upon the King's Death; so that the Nuns

Vindic. of th Sincer. of th Prot. Relig. p. 66, 67.

contended vigorously among themselves who should be Abbesses in their own Countrey.

At the time of His Majesty's Execution Mr. *Henry Spotswood*, riding casually that way, saw a Priest on Horseback in the Habit of a Trouper, with whom he was well acquainted, flourishing his Sword over his Head in triumph as others did; he told Mr. *Spotswood*, that there were at least forty Priests and Jesuites present in the same equipage, among whom was *Preston*, who afterwards commanded a Troup of Horse under *Cromwell*.

Foxes & Firebrands, part 2. p. 86.

Father *Sibthorp*, in a Letter to Father *Metcalfe*, owns that the Jesuites were contrivers of this murther, and that *Sarabras* was present, rejoycing at it; one of the Priests flourishing his Sword, cryed, *Now our greatest Enemy is cut off.*

Vindication of the Prot. Rel. p. 65.

When the News of this Tragedy came to *Roan*, they affirmed, that they had often warned his Majesty, that if he did not establish the Romish Religion in *England*, they should be forced to take such courses as would tend to his Destruction; and now they had kept their words with him: And in *Paris* a Lady having been perverted from the Reformed Church by a Jesuite, upon hearing her Ghostly Father affirm, that now the Catholicks were rid of their greatest Enemy, by whose Death their Cause was much advanced, and therefore she had no reason to lament, left that bloudy and rebellious Church, and continues a Protestant ever since.

H. p. 58. 66.

But though, as Secretary *Morris* affirms, there are almost convincing evidences, that the Papists Irreligion was chiefly guilty of the murther of that excellent Prince; yet we are beholden to the guilty Consciences of those Gentlemen, that the World hath not been long since more fully satisfied, as to every particular; for Dr. *Du Moulin* in the first Edition of his Book

In his Letter to Dr. *du Moulin*, Aug. 9. 1673. *Idem*. p. 54.

Anno 1648.

Anno 1648.

Book *Ann.* 1662. had challenged them to call him to an Account for affirming, that the Rebellion was raised and promoted, and the King murthered by the Arts of the Court of *Rome*; the Book came to a fourth Edition, in all which he renewed the Challenge, and in the laſt in theſe words: *I have defied them now ſeventeen years to call me in queſtion before our Judges, and ſo I do ſtill*; affirming that certain Evidence of what he aſſerted ſhould be produced whenever Authority ſhall require it. *Ib.* p. 61, &c.

I remember once a Jeſuite attempted to prove the truth of the Nag's-Head Ordination, becauſe that Charge had been laid to our Church ſome years before any offered to confute it, or to produce the *Lambeth* Record, which he affirmed was an evident ſign that the thing was true, or elſe having ſuch means to confute it they would not have been ſo long ſilent; what then may we think of thoſe Gentlemen who had ſo heavy a crime charged on them, and yet for near twenty years together never called the Accuſer to account? *Id.* p. 60.

The Doctour always refuſed to produce his Evidences, till required by Authority; only he gives us this Account, That the Papers of Reſolution in favour of the Murther, when it was found to be generally deteſted, were by the Pope's Order gathered up and burnt; but a Roman Catholick in *Paris* refuſed to deliver one in his poſſeſſion, but ſhewed it to a Proteſtant Friend, and related to him the whole carriage of the Negotiation. And I am ſure if the Proteſtants had been under ſuch an Imputation, the Papiſts would make good uſe of their ſilence to prove their Guilt.

But farther to ſhew their averſion to the Royal party, no ſooner had the Rebels of *Ireland*, in conſideration of the ſtraits they were in, made a ceſſation for some time with the Lord *Inchequin*, but the Nuncio excommunicated all who observed it; and upon the conclusion of a second Peace with the Duke of *Ormond*, His Majesty's Lieutenant, the Assembly of the Bishops and Clergy at *James-Town* renounced it, and as much as in them lay, restored the former confederacy anew; but of this we shall have a farther account in its due place.

Anno 1648.

See the Excommunication in the Appendix to the Hist. of the Irish Rem. p. 34.

Walsh's Letters in the Pref.

In the mean while *Reilly*, Vicar General to the A. B. of *Dublin*, betrayed the Royal Camp of *Rathmines* to Coll. *Jones*, Governour of *Dublin* for the Parliament, which service he afterwards pleaded for himself to the safety of his Life, which was in danger for his cruel Actions in the Rebellion, and he well deserved more than bare safety from those men, that defeat being the total ruine of His Majesty's Affairs in *Ireland*.

1649.

Hist. of the Irish Remon. p. 6:9.

At the same time the Rebels in *France* encreased both in Insolence and Power daily, the Coadjutour of *Paris* going to St. *Germains*, in obedience to the Queens Commands, was tumultuously stopt by the People, who hindered the Nobility from following the King, and broke their Coaches; the Parliament forbad all places to receive any Garisons from the King, listed men, and resolved upon a War; the Duke *D'Elbeafe*, Duke of *Lonqueirlle*, Prince *Marsilliack*, afterwards D. of *Rochfecault*, the Prince of *Conty*, and many other persons of the greatest Quality joining with them. Soon after *Normandy* and *Poictou* declared for the Parisians, who sent Deputies to call in the Spaniards to assist them; but these Troubles being in a little time appeased, new ones began in *Provence*, and *Guienne*, the Parliaments of those Provinces, prosecuting the War with great fury, declared they would have no pardon from the King; and one *Gage*, a Priest, endeavoured to persuade

Priorato's Hist. of France, p. 49, &c.

suade them to take the Sovereign Power on themselves, which they declined; but to maintain the War they treated with the Spaniards for Affiftance, both of Men and Moneys.

This Year the Prince of *Conde* joined himself to the *Troudeurs*, which was the ufual Nickname of the difcontented Party; but finding that they intended the advancement of *Chafteau Neuf*, his mortal Enemy, he left them in difguft; however the Parifians made feveral Infurrections; and upon the Imprifonment of that Prince an open Rebellion broke out in *Berry*, whofe Example was followed by *Normandy*, and *Burgundy*, to fupport which the Spaniards agreed to contribute 2000 Foot, and 3000 Horfe, befides great Summes of Money; and foon after the Parliament of *Bourdeaux* declared for the Rebells. *Id.* p. 117, &c.

During thefe Tranfactions the Popifh Bifhops of *Ireland* met at *James-Town*, publifhed a Declaration againft all that fhould adhere to the D. of *Ormond*, His Majefty's Lord-Lieutenant in that Kingdom; upon which my † Authour makes this remark, that if the Archbifhops, &c. in *Ireland* will take upon them to declare againft the King's Authority where His Majefty hath placed it, they affume an Authority to themfelves that no other Clergy ever pretended to, and declare fufficiently to the King, how far they are from being Subjects, or intend to pay him any Obedience longer than they are governed in fuch manner, and by fuch Perfons as they think fit to be pleafed with. See it at large, a d the Duke's Anfwer to it, Hift. of the Irifh Remonft. Ap. p. 65. † Hift. of the Irifh Rebell. p. 261.

But not fatisfied with refufing Obedience to the King's Commiffioner, the Confederates agreed, that if compounding with the Parliament fhould be beft for the People they fhould doe it: And prefently after the Marquefs of *Clauricard* had at their requeft *Id.* p. 276.

taken

taken the Government upon him in his Majesty's Name, it was proposed in their Assembly, that they might send to the Enemy to treat with them upon surrendring all that was left into their hands.

Thus did they chuse rather to submit to the Parliament, than obey the King, for they were not forced to that Submission; the army of the Enemy having made no progress at that time, neither had it been flusht with any new Success.

<small>Vindic. of the Prot. Relig. p. 69.</small>

As forward was Father *Bret* to persuade the Gentlemen who had defended the Castle of *Jersey* for the King, to renounce the Royal Family, and Kingly Government, by taking the Engagement; affirming, that they were not to acknowledge any Supreme but the prevailing Power.

<small>Priorato's Hist. of France, p. 245, 285, 308, 333.</small>

All this while the Rebellion in *France* increased, the Parisians took Arms, designing to seize the King; and the Prince of *Conde* fortified several places, and confederated with the Spaniards, whom, under the Conduct of the Duke of *Nemours*, he called into *France* to his Assistance, with which he maintained the War all this Year, to whom the Duke of *Orleance* joined himself, and with all his Interest increased the Party.

<small>Long's Hist. of Plots, p. 15, 16.</small>

<small>Vindic. of the Prot. Relig. p. 67, &c.</small>

The next year Mr. *Tho. White* published his Book of the Grounds of Obedience and Government, wherein he asserts, That if a Prince governs ill he becomes a Robber, and the People may expell him, in which case they are not bound by any Promise made to him; and that they have no Obligation to endeavour the Restauration of a Prince so dispossessed of his Dominions, but rather to hinder it; nay, though he were wrongfully driven out; and such a Prince is absolutely obliged to renounce all Right and Claim to the Government; and if he doth not, he is worse than an Infidel. Thus after their Designs

Anno 1652. signs had effected the death of that good King, and expulsion of his late and present Majesty, they contributed their Endeavours to hinder their return, and debauch those who might attempt it; yet had some the confidence to commend this Gentleman to his late Majesty, though the King knew him too well to take any notice of him.

That they designed to hinder the Restauration of the King, by an absolute compliance with the usurping Power, is affirmed by one of their Communion, who tells them that they were refractory to the Queen's Desires at *Rome* for His Majesty's Assistance, and that Collonel *Hutchinson* could discover strange Secrets about their treating with *Cromwell*. Jesuites Reasons unreasonable, p. 103, 104.

And it is certain that in *Ireland* there were several Precepts granted by the Archbishop of *Armagh*, and others, to pray for the success of that Usurper's Forces; while *Dominick Decupsy*, a Dominican, esteemed a Person of great Holiness, and *Long*, the Jesuite, asserted, that the King being out of the Roman Church, it was not lawfull to pray for him particularly, or publickly on any other day except Good Fryday, as comprehended among the Infidels and Hereticks; and then only for the spiritual Welfare of his Soul, not for his temporal prosperity. Hist. of Irish Rebellion, p. 241.

The Civil Wars continuing still in *France*, our present Sovereign, then Duke of *York*, went into the King's Army; and the Princes being straitened, called in the Duke of *Lorrain*, who with his Army marched to their Succour, so that they kept the Field all this and the ensuing Year. *Priorato*'s Hist. of *France*, p. 358, &c.

1654. *Anno* 1654. there was a Discourse written by *Benoist de Treglies*, Collateral of the Council, or Regent of the Chancery of *Naples*, in which this Proposition was maintained, *That when a Pope intends to exercise any Jurisdiction in a Countrey, he ought to* St. Amour's Annals, p. 448. let

let his Writs be examined by the temporal Prince, that so it may be known whether the Causes and Persons contained therein be of his Jurisdiction: Which Proposition having been examined by the Inquisition at *Rome,* at the express command of the Pope, that Congregation declared it to be Heretical and Schismatical, prohibiting the Book, and threatening the severest censures against the Authour. {Anno 1654.}

The following year affords us a farther evidence of the hopes the Romanists had conceived of the restauration of their Religion here; for Dr. *Baily,* at the end of the Life of *Fisher,* Bishop of *Rochester,* speaking of the Lord *Cromwell,* and the great influence he had upon the proceedings in the beginning of the Reformation, expresses their hopes of his Party from the Usurper, and his Counsels, in these words: *Who knows but that the Church may be healed of her Wounds by the same Name, sithence the Almighty hath communicated so great a Secret unto Mortals as that there should be such a Salve made known to them, whereby the same Weapon that made the Wound should work the Cure.* Oliva vera *is not so hard to be construed* Oliverus, *as that it may not be believed that a Prophet, rather than a Herald, gave the common Father of Christendom, the now Pope of* Rome, (Innocent X.) *such Ensigns of his Nobility,* (viz. *a Dove holding an Olive Branch in her mouth,*) *since it falls short in nothing of being a Prophesie, and fulfilled, but only his Highness running into her Arms, whose Embleme of Innocence bears him already in her mouth.* {Baily's Life of Fisher, p. 260, 261. London, 1655. 8vo.} {1655.}

Three years after this Popish Loyal Flattery, Father *Ferrall,* a Capuchin, presented a Treatise to the Cardinals of the Congregation, *de Propaganda Fide,* proposing some Methods to revive the Rebellion in *Ireland,* and drive out not only the English, but also all the Irish who were descended from the old En- {Hist. of the Irish Remonst. p. 740.} {1658.}

Anno 1658. glish Conquerours, as not fit to be trusted in so holy a League; and about the same time Father *Reiley, the Popish Primate, coming through *Brussels*, refused to kiss the King's Hand, though some offered to introduce him: And to obtain favour with

* The same who had betrayed Rathmines to Jones.

1659. Richard Cromwell, he alledged that the Irish Natives had no affection to the King, and his Family; and therefore were fit to be trusted by the Protectour; and upon his Arrival in *Ireland*, he made it his business to gain a party there to hinder the King's Restauration, promising them great assistance; upon which the King gave notice of those Contrivances to *Don Stephano de Gamarro*, the Spanish Ambassadour, in *Holland*, so that he was recalled to *Rome*, to avoid the danger of the Law.

Hist. of the Irish Remon. p. 610.

And (which is a farther Evidence of the Enmity of that party to the Royal Family) when General *Monk* was at *London*, in prosecution of that great and good Design which he afterwards completed, and had by his prudent Conduct gained the Affections of the People *Monsieur de Bourdeaux*, the French Ambassadour, told Mr. *Clergis*, † *That Cardinal Mazarine would be glad to have the Honour of his Friendship, and would assist him faithfully in all his Enterprises; and that the General might be more confident of the Cardinal, he assured him that* Oliver Cromwell *kept so strict a League with him, that he did not assume the Government without his Privity, and was directed step by step by him, in the progress of that Action; and therefore if he resolved on that course, he should not only have the Cardinal's Friendship and Counsel in the Attempt, but a safe Retreat, and honourable Support in* France, *if he failed in it*.

Long's Hist. of Plots, p. 87, 88.

1662. Soon after His Majesty's Restauration, which all the Contrivances of these men could not hinder, the Jesuites presented a Paper to several persons of Honour,

Honour, pleading to be included within a favourable Vote which had been made with reference to all other Romanists; in which they acknowledge, that no party in their Church think the Deposing Doctrine sinfull, but themselves, who are by Order of their General forbidden to meddle with it: But, as their Answerer observes, this makes them but the more guilty, seeing their Loyalty depends upon the Will of their General, which is all they pretend to be influenced by in this matter: But this is not all, for they impose upon the World in that Assertion, there being no such Decree which respects any other Countrey but *France*; and whereas (if we should grant them that) they pretend to be bound by it under pain of Damnation, this likewise is false; for none of their Constitutions oblige them under so much as a Venial Sin.

Therefore the same person advised them to join in a Subscription of Abhorrence of those Deposing Doctrines, which had been too often maintained by them; but this was a piece of Loyalty to which they could never arrive.

The former year some of the Irish Clergy and Gentry, to make some amends for their Rebellion, had subscribed that Declaration which Mr. *Cressy* published in the year 1647. which hath since been called the Irish Remonstrance, and made a great noise in the World for some years; for no sooner was an Account of this Loyal Action transmitted to *Rome*, but the Internuncio *De Vecchiis*, then Resident at *Brussels*, by the Pope's Order declared, that his Holiness had condemned it; and Cardinal *Barberini*, in a Letter to the Noblemen of *Ireland*, affirmed, that such as subscribe it do, to shew their Fidelity to the King, destroy their Faith; and therefore exhorted all to beware of those Seducers who pro-

Marginalia:
Jesuites Reasons unreasonable, p. 112, &c.

id. p. 127.

Hist. of the Irish Remon. p. 16, 17, 18. Where see the Letters, and p. 513, 514.

Anno 1662.

Anno 1662.	promoted the Subscriptions to it, and † Father *Ma-cedo*, a *Portugueze*, who had formerly made a Latine Panegyrick upon *Cromwell*, was employed to write against it. The *Dominicans refused absolution to some of their Order, because they would not retract their Approbations; and the Provincial box'd another for the same cause; † The Augustinians absolutely refused to sign it; so did the ‖ Franciscans, * and * the Jesuites. †*Anthony Mac Gheoghegan*, Popish Bishop of *Meath*, and several others, sent Father *John Brady* to *Rome*, to get a direct Censure published against it: And the Theological Faculty at ‖*Lovain*, declared that it contained many things contrary to the Catholick Faith, and ought not to be signed by any; But Father *Shelton*, and several other Priests, were more particular, who told Father *Walsh*, the Procurator for the Irish Clergy in this Affair, ‖ that they would not subscribe that form, nor any other, denying a power in the Pope to depose the King, or absolve Subjects from their Allegiance, because this is a matter of right, controverted between two great Princes.	‖ *M*. p. 43. † p. 54. ‖ p. 49. * p. 60. † p. 91. ‖ p. 102. ‖ p. 84.
1664.	Two years after † *de Riddere*, Commissary General of the Franciscans for the Belgick Provinces, in a National Congregation of all the Provincials of that Order subject to him, declared the Subscribers of the Remonstrance to be Schismaticks, reserving a Power to their Superiours to proceed against them when it should be convenient.	† p. 116.
1665.	And the Nuncio *de Vecchiis*, in a Letter to Father *Caron*, calls the Remonstrance a Rock of Offence; but the Bishop of * *Ferns* he declared himself more positively for the Deposing Power in his Letter to Dr. *James Cusack*, *Jun*. 18. 1662. and therefore in his Letter to the ‖ D. of *Ormond*, *Sep*. 22. this year, he justifies all that was done at *James-Town* by the	‖ p. 531. * p. 617, &c. ‖ p. 620, 629.

Romish

Romish Bishops, who broke the Peace of 1648. and two years after they excommunicated the Duke, then His Majesty's Lieutenant there, refusing to obey him any longer.

† p. 624, &c.
And the same Bp. in two † Letters to Father *Walsh* the next year, seriously professed that he durst not renounce the Pope's Deposing Power, which was maintained by 7 *Saints*, *(St.* Thomas *one,)* 7 *Cardinals*, 1 *Patriarch*, 3 *A.Bps.* 10 *Bps.* and 31 *Classical Authors*, *with other eminent Divines* ; and chose rather to continue a banisht man, than declare against them.

Anno 1666.

* p. 533.
† p. 634.
And when His Majesty had granted liberty to the R. Clergy of that Nation to hold a national Synod that year, to try if they would give any assurance of their Loyalty, * Card. *Barberini* wrote to them not to subscribe that Protestation; and the † Internuncio *Rospigliosi* affirmed, that to sign the Remonstrance rendered the Subscribers Instruments of the Damnation of others.

* Ld. Clarend. against *Cressy*, p. 247, 248.
*. The Cardinal minded them that the Kingdom remained under Excommunication, and therefore advised them to consider what they did.

Hist. of the Irish Remonst. p. 647, &c.
At length the Assembly met, and the Card. sent Letters dissuading them to give any such assurance of their Loyalty, as being prejudicial to the Cath. Faith, which was seconded by another from the Internuncio, and the Bp. of *Ipres*, directed to some of the Synod, who were very obedient to these Admonitions; for when Father *Walsh* endeavoured to prove that several great Divines had opposed the Deposing Doctrine,

† p. 657.
† Father *Nettervile* interrupted him, affirming that none had asserted the contrary, but a Schismatical Historian, and a Poet, meaning *Sigibertus Gemblacensis*, and *Dantes Aligherius* ;

* p. 666.
* soon after which they resolved not only not to sign the Remonstrance, but not to suffer it to be read in the House: And when the Procuratour desired them to beg his Majesty's

Anno 1666. sty's Pardon for the late execrable Rebellion, *they not only refused to ask pardon but so much as to acknowledge there was any need of it*; affirming publickly *that they knew none at all guilty of any Crime for any thing done in the War*. And when the Lord Lieutenant desired them to give his Majesty some assurance of their future Obedience, *in case of any Deposition or Excommunication from the Pope, they refused even this without so much as putting it to the Question*.

* *Id.* Pref. p. 3, 4.

They offered indeed several Forms instead of the Remonstrance, but in none of them renounced the Deposing Power; in that the Assembly signed at their breaking up, they disowned the Doctrine, but would not declare that Doctrine which abetts it unsound and sinfull; wherein they have been imitated by some late Writers, who though called upon to affirm it such, never did it.

Idem p. 763.

Once indeed they seemed to come something near what was expected, when their *Chairman told Father *Walsh*, *That it was not out of any prejudice against the Remonstrance they would not sign it, but because they thought it more becoming their Dignity and Liberty to word their own sense; for the rest, they were far from condemning that Remonstrance or the Subscribers thereof*: Yet would they not own this when desired under their Hands, but refused; so that no good being expected, they were dissolved, leaving an undeniable Evidence of their aversion to Loyalty, and approbation of the treasonable Doctrine of the Ch. of *Rome*.

* p. 675.

Soon after the Dissolution of this Synod the E. of *Sandwich*, Ambassadour in *Spain*, informed His Majesty that Primate *Reilly* was emplyed to stir up his Countrey-men to rebell, upon which a Gurd was set upon him, and in a little time was sent into *France*.

p. 746.

1674. The Bp. of *Ferns* still justified the Rebellion, defending the Actions of the Clergy for *laudable, vertuous,*

Walsh's Letter p. 54.

tuous, meritorious Deeds, and becoming good Men; and therefore needing no Repentance: And this is the last Account I find of him, for he soon after dyed.

And now the Controversie about the *Regale* growing hot between the King of *France* and the present Pope, His Holiness had so much of the Spirit of his Predecessours, who were for asserting their Power over all the Kingdoms of the World, as to threaten the King with Excommunication, and that speedily, if he would not renounce his Claim, and he was as good as his word; for the King not being affraid of his Thunders, and refusing to lose his Right, and the Assembly of the Clergy joining with his Majesty, the Pope sent a Bull of Excommunication to his Nuncio, requiring him to publish it in the Assembly; but by the diligence of the Cardinal *d'Estree*, the Assembly was adjourned before the Arrival of the Bull.

News from France, p. 37. Lond. 1682. 4to.

At the same time *Szlepeche*, my Primate of *Hungary*, with his Clergy, maintained the Deposing Power, by a Censure of the contrary Opinion; and the next year the Spanish Inquisition at *Toledo* did the same; which was followed three years after by four *Theses*, publickly maintained by the Jesuites at their College of *Clermont* in *Auvergne*, wherein it was defended; and even among our selves the Authour of Popery Anatomised defends the Decree of the Council of *Laterane*, in that the Kings and Princes of *Europe* by their Ambassadours consented to it, affirming that the Christian World apprehended no injury, but rather security in that Decree.

Walsh's Letters in the Pref.

Popery Anat. p. 14. Lond. 1636. 4to.

Anno
1679.
1682.
1687.
1686.

FINIS.

Advertisement of two other Books writ by the Authour of this Book.

1. THE Missionaries Arts discovered: or, an Account of their Ways of Insinuation, their Artifices, and several Methods of which they serve themselves in making Converts to the Church of *Rome*. With a Letter to *A Fulion*.

2. A Plain Defence of the Protestant Religion, fitted to the meanest Capacity, being a full Answer to the Popish Net for the Fishers of Men, that was writ by two Converts; wherein is evidently made appear, that their Departure from the Protestant Religion was without Cause or Reason. Fit to be read by all Protestants.

www.ingramcontent.com/pod-product-compliance
Lightning Source LLC
Chambersburg PA
CBHW020149170426
43199CB00010B/953